Wounded Wings
A Lesbian Journey
of Love and Loss

Wounded Wings
A Lesbian Journey of Love and Loss

BY ELIZABETH KIDWELL

Chatter House Press
Indianapolis, Indiana

Wounded Wings
A Lesbian Journey of Love and Loss

Copyright© 2019 by Elizabeth Kidwell
Cover Art by EVE

All rights reserved.

Except for brief quotations embodied in critical articles and reviews in newspapers, magazines, radio or television, no part of this book may be reproduced in any form or by any means electronic, mechanical, or by any information storage and retrieval system without written permission from the publisher.

For information:

Chatter House Press
7915 S Emerson Ave, Ste B303
Indianapolis, IN 46237

chatterhousepress.com

ISBN: 978-1-937793-51-7

Dedication

To my mother Jeanne,
who gave me life
and then gave it to me again 27 years later

To my mother Josephine,
who taught me to have a life
and then told me to write about it

To my mother Joanne,
who taught me that life is all about love

and

To my beloved Emilia,
who combined life and love in a most magical way

Contents

Dedication	v
Gathering	1
Shipwrecked	3
Life Roads	7
Tail Shaker	11
Invasion	19
Soldier Girl	25
Grappled	31
Suicide Hill	37
Pumpkin	45
Fallen	53
Hair	61
Scars	71
Dancing Rainbows	79
Riptide	89
Moon Woman	97
Winter Solstice	107
Breath	117
Clothed	125
General	131
Stroke	143
Inflight	157
Natural Process	167
Midnight Sun	177
Restored	183
Postcards	191
Showered	203
No Words	211

Chapter 1
Gathering

You take the night away from me
And give me brightest day.
You gather all my wonderings
And bid me gently, stay.

You take my fractured pieces,
The puzzle that you see,
And shape me into wholeness,
Then softly set me free.

You wrap your love around me
And show me how to grow.
You melt my heart on contact
And teach me all you know.

You make your life a gift to me.
You could not give me more.
You found my house with windows shut,
Yet opened up my door.

And now I give myself to you;
I'm all I have to share.
I put my life into your keep,
My heart within your care.

I have a home inside of you;
There is no lock or key.
The furnishings are simple:
It is filled with you and me.

Wounded Wings

Chapter 2
Shipwrecked

Though I could describe the wonders and magic of Mother Earth where Emi and I fully lived during the twenty-five years we shared our lives, this book is really about my loss of her. I had no idea what real pain felt like until she took her last breath. The life that drained from her, drained from me as well. For the next year and more, I lived with a stranger, a hollow person, my empty self. The joyous memories of our love and life together now came flooding back to echo in lost spaces and to haunt me. My desire to remember and to relive our happy times was thwarted by a deep loneliness. I cried every day.

My youngest sister Louise flew out from California twice in the first two months of my mourning period, the night of Emi's death and again during the week that included Emi's memorial service. Nothing had changed in me during the month between her flights. I still cried every day. Louise warned me, "Ellie, if you keep crying like this, you will get pink eye."

Her words jolted me out of my sad thoughts. "What?" I asked. Then she explained that a woman she knew had developed pink eye by crying all the time after her husband divorced her.

"It's not the same thing," I argued.

"A loss is a loss," she countered.

After my sister returned home, I ignored her warning and kept up my sobbing and wailing. I just could not help it. Everything in the house set me off. It had become for me a museum to Emi's memory. Each room contained countless belongings that had meaning for us.

Worried that pink eye could be on the horizon, I finally performed my first sensible act. I searched the Internet for a lesbian grief therapist, who might be able to help me turn off the tears. Finding one named Ellen, I dialed her number. A woman with a kind voice answered the phone.

"My name is Ellie, short for Elizabeth," I explained. "My partner of twenty-five years recently died, and I can't stop crying. Is there an appropriate waiting period before seeking help for my grief?"

The voice that answered me sounded gently amused. "No, there isn't. It is when you feel you need help. Would you like to make an appointment to see me?"

"Yes," I sobbed and burst into tears.

Three days later I sat in Ellen's office as she encouraged me to tell her about Emi and how she died. I did so, crying the whole time. "The therapy is not working," I apologized.

"Give it some time," she suggested. "Don't be so hard on yourself."

By my third session I began bringing Ellen poems that I had written in the interim, in which I poured out my grief as well as my tears. I wanted to share how wonderful my Love had been and the beautiful life we shared. Each poem had washed out of me in a deluge of tears, as painful as ripping a scab off an old wound.

In this first poem, I tried to tell about an exciting birding trip we had taken many years ago to Machias Seal Island, a Canadian bird refuge between the Bay of Fundy and the Gulf of Maine in the Atlantic Ocean. There, we saw nesting Arctic terns, razorbills, and Atlantic puffins. All three were lifer birds for both of us. However, the words of the poem did not reflect the joy and excitement of that trip as I had intended.

Elizabeth Kidwell

Lost at sea, I am
Barely able to keep my head above water,
Adrift with no compass,
Hopelessly abandoned in endless ocean,
Not even a whale for company,
I lie back and let the waves
Carry me where they will.

The sky above me is vast emptiness,
Too much blue.
I add my salty tears to the restless,
Immeasurable brine,
And the drops are hardly noticed.
It would be so easy
To roll over and surrender myself
To the cold loneliness.

When once before we traveled
The frigid Atlantic,
We had a boat, companions,
A dingy for safe passage through the fog.

The island was a place of wonder:
Treasure, birds flapping all around us: Life.

Wounded Wings

Now, having abandoned ship,
I have no captain, no navigator,
No star to mark my passage,
No port, no calm,
Just raging seas in my heart,
And an insistent current
Tugging me under.
I have no anchor.

Chapter 3
Life Roads

One day early in our partnership, Emi arrived home with a brand new road map of North America. Triumphantly, she opened it to show me. "What's that for?" I asked, curiously amused.

She smiled and explained, "This is our new life road map. Every road we travel together we'll highlight! Then, we'll have a visual memory of all our travels. There will be many, Ellie," she vowed.

Emi was true to her word. Already retired from teaching, she eagerly awaited my breaks from school. Each summer vacation and every fall, spring, and Christmas break found us journeying to incredibly beautiful locations all over the United States and Canada, special places Emi wanted to enjoy again through my eyes. With her first partner Beth, she had traveled to exotic locations in Europe, Africa, the Galápagos Islands, Canada, and Hawaii. Now as Emi aged, we planned our trips closer to our home in Indiana. We adventured in New England, the Southwest, the Dakotas, and practically every state, often more than once. We even enjoyed two stays in our nation's Capital, a place with which Emi was extremely familiar, as I was eventually to discover.

Often, we combined many of our journeys with Elderhostels, special programs for older adults over fifty-five. I wasn't old enough to qualify, but because I was a companion to an elderly person, I was allowed to attend. Emi acted sufficiently helpless, and I was in! Later on, it wasn't an act, but we still enjoyed our travels and classes with some pretty memorable seniors from all over the U.S. and Canada.

Rainbow-like, our Life Map came alive as year after year, Emi marked the roads to and from every destination with a colored highlighter. The map became magically beautiful and proudly displayed!

When Emi entered her 70's, it was obvious to me that she was slowing down a little. Neuropathy had developed in her legs and feet, making it more difficult for her to walk comfortably, and so she began to use a cane. In addition, I had just spent a year recovering from a complete hysterectomy to cure my doctor's diagnosis of uterine cancer. Perhaps, we both felt a sense of urgency to add to our Life Map.

One day in early spring, I asked Emi, "Is there a place you have always wanted to see and have never been?"

She didn't hesitate. "Alaska!" she replied. "I've always wanted to go to Alaska."

"Then that will be the perfect destination for our summer vacation!" I exclaimed. "Why don't you get some travel books from our agent, and we can plan this trip together." Within days, Emi brought home every book and pamphlet available on Alaska from our local Triple A outlet and even more from our travel agent. I arrived home from school the next afternoon to find my grinning Emi seated at the dining room table, which was covered with colorful brochures! She had the whole trip planned within a week!

As it turned out, our trip of a lifetime to Alaska combined a ten-day cruise on the old Holland America ship, the *Rotterdam*, a week-long inland excursion including a train trip on the McKinley Explorer to marvel at the majestic, snow-capped Denali, and a bus trip to Fairbanks. We crowned our journey with an airplane ride in a World War II, twin-engine plane over the Bering Sea to the island of St. Paul in the Pribilofs. As part of a special week-long Elderhostel, we were guests of the Aleut people, who inhabited the island. They were wonderful teachers as they explained their history, culture, and art. They also took us on field trips in a small blue bus to explore the island, where the tallest tree, a willow, was only six inches high. Wonders on the island included fur seals, who hauled out on the shore to breed; Arctic foxes, who had spent the summer shedding their white winter fur in favor of black; a herd of domestic caribou, and various lifer birds including a wheatear from nearby Siberia! Emi didn't need to see anything through my eyes this time because hers were wide open with delight the whole trip!

No matter where we journeyed together, Emi always mailed me at least one postcard from each destination, a special message which would be waiting for me when we returned home. It was such a sweet

Elizabeth Kidwell

custom, and I looked forward to the picture she would choose to send. On the back of the postcard, the sentiment was ever the same, "So you will remember our time together. Love always, Emi."

This trip she had sent me a postcard of that majestic mountain, Denali, and for the first time, upon our return home, Emi stood very close when she handed that postcard to me from the pile of mail. When I turned it over, I was surprised to see two additional sentences. They read, "Sweetheart, I have breast cancer. I didn't tell you sooner because I wanted you to enjoy our trip." She was a wise woman to stand next to me because she had to support me in her arms as I dissolved into tears.

True to tradition, the next day Emi took out our Life Map. Despite my sadness about her impending surgery, I was curious to see how she would mark it. She worked on it for quite some time, and when she finished, she proudly displayed her workmanship. Along the coast from Vancouver, B.C. to Juneau, she had used a dark blue marker to indicate the "road" our ship had taken along the Pacific coast.

For the train trip to Denali, she had used a green highlighter to trace the train tracks to Denali National Park and our inland bus passage to Fairbanks. For our flight to St. Paul and back, she had drawn broken lines in purple to represent the plane trip to the Pribilofs.

Then, she folded the Life Map, took my hands in her own, and looked lovingly into my eyes. "Our next journey together," she commented bravely, "will not be on this map."

In response, I enfolded her in my arms and held on tight. Softly into her ear, I whispered with love, "I will be with you every step of the way."

Wounded Wings

You called them "life roads,"
Those highways that carried us both to adventure,
The carefully-marked map tracing the routes.

How eagerly and happily we prepared to be amazed
At the life that blessed every destination, each new road
Beckoning us on to unforgettable places!

Our eyes relished the beauty and the wonder
Of creation unknown and sometimes off the map,
But we were never lost, and though far away, always home.

So what is this unfamiliar road that I must travel now?
Have I made a wrong turn? Gone off the map?
This trip we never planned has no destination.

Where am I going without you?
There are no markers, no familiar signs of life,
No light to show me the way.

I cannot see the road ahead of me;
Not so sure that it leads anywhere
I want to go. Which way do I turn now?

This cannot be a life road if I am traveling Alone.
Where is the "beautiful path" that leads me home
To you? Surely, I am lost.

Chapter 4
Tail Shaker

Because Emi was so much older than I, she had often spoken of the possibility that she would die before me. Having lost the love of her life who was only ten years her senior, she wanted to prepare me, but I dreaded the mere thought of living without her, and I would just burst into tears. So she was surprised when I asked her a strange question as we lay together in bed, happy in each other's arms one lazy Sunday morning. "Emi," I began, getting her attention.

"Yes, Darling," she responded, focusing on me completely as she always did, making me feel as if I were the only person in her world.

"If you die before I do, and if it is at all possible in the spirit world, will you come back and let me know that you are all right?"

Immediately, Emi propped herself up on her elbow and turned to look at me, obviously amused. Her soft, brown eyes suddenly blazed like candles in a jack-o'-lantern and her grin was just as wide. She placed her face lovingly against mine, looked into my eyes, and promised, "I'll do better than that! I'll HAUNT you!" She laughed and gathered me close, and we made love, sweet and tender.

In the days following Emi's death, I became a hermit. Louise stayed with me for ten days and then flew home to her family. I tried to resume my everyday life, but I didn't have one. I had retired just twenty-seven days before Emi died with the intention of finally spending more time with her. She had waited for twenty-five years for me to retire completely and to become her constant companion, and when I finally was able to, I lost her.

Besides, when Emi died, I wasn't the only one who grieved. Our little five-pound female Maltese, Squirt, also mourned her loss. Squirt had been given to us by a neighbor just three years before when she was six months old, yappy and uncontrollable. Emi and I had taken care of her on weekends since she was ten weeks old while our neighbor worked at a nearby hospital. The first time we cared for the puppy, we were amazed at her tiny size. "What a little squirt!" Emi exclaimed, and while that was not the name our neighbor had given the pup, we never called her anything else and the name just stuck. We were also surprised that a tiny dog could emit such a deafening bark! Under my firm hand and Emi's gentle one, Squirt settled down happily, quickly adapting to our simple routine and becoming a special member of our pack. By this time Emi was almost eighty-five, and her neuropathy was so advanced that she spent many peaceful days sitting comfortably in her "electric chair," as we dubbed her lift chair. I would cover her with a light fleece blanket and there in the center of the cover, I would deposit Squirt, lap dog and queen. Emi always kept one hand lovingly on Squirt's soft, warm body, petting her absentmindedly while she read or watched television. When Emi happened to lift her hand to turn a page, one backward glance from Squirt reminded her of its proper place. Often the two of them slept companionably for an hour or two.

When Emi failed to return home from the hospital that last time, Squirt went searching for her, and I tracked behind anxiously. She looked in her bedroom, sniffing in every corner and gazing up at her bed where I had lifted her every morning as soon as Emi awoke. She would also inspect her bathroom, placing her paws against the bathtub, snuffling hopefully. Squirt searched under Emi's desk and chair in the living room, and under and on her chair at the kitchen table, before finally ending her quest at Emi's electric chair. I followed Squirt's sad journey like a lost lamb, crying hopelessly. Every day I placed Squirt on my lap and cried more bitter tears, soaking her tiny, snow-white, furry back because my heart was broken. It was our grieving time together, and I know that Squirt understood our loss as much as I did, and I shed tears for the both of us because she couldn't. One day I even took Squirt with me for my grief therapy session because I was positive that she was depressed also. Ellen understood and welcomed Squirt, too.

Eventually, I left the house and walked to the grocery store just two blocks away, but the autumn sun burned so brightly that I couldn't stand it. It blinded me. Inside the Safeway, the customers acted as if the end of the world had not occurred at all. They were talking, laughing, buying groceries. Their voices and faces registered too much life. I was uncomfortable and left without buying anything.

Eventually, I decided just to stay home, secure, but then I realized that everywhere I looked inside the house lay objects that tortured my soul with sweet memories. Ultimately, I decided that the best place to be was at Emi's desk in the living room looking out the two windows facing the backyard. That way I didn't have to see anything in the house and nobody could see me. The desk was completely cleared on top and polished thanks to Louise's first visit, and I brought my new iPad, another gift from my sweet sister, and placed it in the center. Next, I touched the icon for Kindle, where she had thoughtfully loaded dozens of books.

Hesitantly, I browsed through the titles, searching for an eBook that would take me away from my sad world and into another where I wouldn't have to cry and grieve. The title *Fifty Shades of Grey* caught my eye. I remembered that it was the first book in a trilogy recommended by my dear friend Ann. So trustingly, I began to read, gazing periodically into the heavily-wooded backyard that offered shade and privacy. Needless to say, the book kept my attention! The world of the book was perfect; it had nothing to do with my own life and loss.

For the next two weeks my world became predictably robotic. Sleep restlessly, poorly: cry. Try to eat a meal: cry. Feed Squirt: cry. Hold Squirt: cry, soaking her again and clinging to her tiny warm body for comfort. Only when I sat at Emi's desk and read, did the tears stop. When I chanced to look outside, robins, cardinals, chickadees, and sparrows foraged for food or sat hungrily stuffing themselves at the bird feeders. I tried not to show interest in their activities or I would cry. Birdwatching was torturous also. Too much life.

If I had not glanced up from my iPad at the exact moment several mornings later, I might have missed her: a small olive-brown bird with a streaked white breast, emerging from under a bush, and bobbing her way across the backyard, heading directly toward my window. I watched mesmerized as she shook her somewhat stubby tail with each step, pausing occasionally to toss a leaf into the air. As she stepped closer, I knew that she was a lifer bird. Definitely some kind of thrush, I thought, as I grabbed my bird identification guide off a nearby shelf, just to be sure. There, on page 387, I found her: a Louisiana Waterthrush with her bubblegum pink legs, distinctive white eyebrows, and a habit of bobbing her tail with each step. Technically, she was a wood warbler, an uncommon bird in Indianapolis, obviously on her southernly migration in mid-September, following the males who had migrated a month earlier. I watched her for quite some time. As I stood up to get a better look, she halted her progress directly under the window, stared up at me for a moment, and bowed. I marked her species on my Life List, fully expecting her to be gone in the morning.

But she wasn't. She remained in the backyard all the next day, and the next, until a week had passed. I could see her out the kitchen window also when I began to eat again. Every morning I figured she'd be gone, but remarkably, she stayed as the days turned into another week. I felt strangely comforted as if Emi were keeping her promise to let me know that she was all right.

Two weeks later, Louise returned from California to help me plan Emi's memorial open house, which coincided with what would have been Emi's eighty-eighth birthday. Through the kitchen picture window I pointed out the waterthrush I had told her about when she had phoned to check up on me. "She's still here," I explained. "It's been three weeks, almost October, and she should have flown away by now."

"I'm just glad that you have stopped crying," my sister commented lovingly, giving the bird an appreciative look.

During the open house at the end of the week, I ushered special friends into the kitchen to see the waterthrush bobbing along the backyard. They were kind if not impressed.

Following the gathering, the guests returned home, and two days later, my sister flew back to California. Once again I resumed my hermit lifestyle, reading at Emi's desk, now pausing frequently to observe the waterthrush, who inexplicably chose to remain.

One quiet morning, I sat at Emi's desk, finishing the last chapter of the book. Shattering the silence, a bird dove directly into the window before me and crashed into it with a bang! Startled that it might be the waterthrush, I rushed outside to discover a hermit thrush lying on its back on the concrete walkway. I stood close to the gray-brown bird and bent down, watching the thrush as it struggled to breathe, its spotted breast rising and falling, its beak wide open, an eerie reminder of Emi's final shallow breaths just over a month ago.

"Please, don't die," I pleaded to the stunned bird, my eyes filling with tears. I stood by the helpless thrush's side for over a half-hour to protect it from harm. Finally, I bent down and in a soft voice, I asked it, "Can you stand?"

As if in response, the thrush, in a single motion, turned over and hopped to its feet. The reclusive bird seemed strangely unafraid of me as I stood just inches away from it. After a short while, I leaned over again and I inquired, "Can you walk?"

In answer, the bird took two steps and hopped off the walkway. Feeling hopeful, I asked one final question, "Can you fly?"

At those words, the hermit thrush flew a short distance into a lower branch of the backyard cherry tree and looked down at me. After a few moments, it flew away, out of my sight.

Stunned by the drama of the bird's crash and recovery, I once again burst into tears, but the message had been delivered, clearly and forcefully: my hermit days were over. Tentatively brave once more, I walked into the front yard to view my perennial garden. There like a blessing, in the mid-October sunshine, on the pink sedum buzzed a large swarm of honey bees, a species that Emi and I had been concerned about and had not seen in the flower garden in five years! Then, a dusky winter wren landed on a coneflower stalk and scolded me, as if he had claimed the garden in my absence. Suddenly, life burst forth all around me, but this time, I was all right with it. Once again, as throughout my life, I felt at home in nature. The thrush's injury and recovery felt like a comforting prognosis for me.

During the next week Emi sent me even more speckled-breasted, shy, woodland birds, two ovenbirds and a pair brown thrashers, while the Louisiana Waterthrush continued her backyard layover. Finally, in the third week of October, the waterthrush bobbed her way to the window again, where I sat already reading the second book of the trilogy. I stood up to see her better. She gazed up at me through the window, bowed in greeting, and stood proudly, her streaked breast large and well-fed. I knew then that she was saying good-bye. Fortified for her journey, she would fly tonight and be gone tomorrow. She had been my daily companion for an astonishing five weeks! Emi was true to her word, I believed. I felt lovingly haunted!

Elizabeth Kidwell

Small, brown bird, tail shaker,
You migrated into my heart years ago.
Now that your spirit has flown,
You have chosen to stay in the backyard,
Not for a day, not for a week,
But for an entire month,
Keeping me company in my great sorrow.

Who whispers to you, suggesting this long layover?
You dance your way across moist ground,
Comically tossing leaves into the air,

Bobbing and bowing as if I were royalty,
Filling your streaked breast with insects,
Journey food for this long, autumn trip.
Oh, my beloved night flyer!

Your presence alone fills my breast with comfort
On this flyway I must travel alone.
Will my heart beat with the rhythm of your soft wings,
And will it ever soar to reach the pinnacle of your life?
You were born to fly, yet here I am, earthbound,
Left behind to endure this barren, frozen winter,
While you seek warm mangroves in a foreign land.

Wounded Wings

Will you return next spring,
When warm rains fall to hasten nature's growth?
Will you find me at the window watching
And quicken my spirit with your inner drive
To return to northern forests and family?
When your migration comes full circle,
I want to be in its center, hovering, balanced.

Chapter 5
Invasion

My Emi was a hoarder. When she finally invited me to move in with her, following my cancer surgery, seven years after we met, it became necessary for me to sell my house and the majority of my furniture because her four-bedroom home was completely filled with a lifetime of gathered belongings. Each item she treasured came fully attached to a priceless story. She had loved three people completely in her life so far: her mother Marie, her father Raymond, and her first partner Beth. Her home was a museum to them: antique furniture, antique dishes, antique memories. Because I loved her, I listened to the stories about the people she loved over and over, fully aware that these special people had helped to mold Emi into the priceless, loving person that she was.

Emi clung tenaciously to everything because of the precious memories of those special people still fully alive in her heart and mind. It was up to me to fit in and to help her create new memories. She was so proud of herself when she cleared out two dressers and one closet in the guest bedroom not too long after her invitation. Such was my great love for her, I made do. "Sardine" was the word that came to mind at the time. Another word, "guest" gave me anxious pause. It was a room I graciously moved out of when we had visitors. Eventually, I bought a new bed for myself and relocated to her thousand-book library upstairs next to the guest room so I would not have to give up my bed each month when visitors arrived. Emi lovingly removed her makeshift library table to make space for my bed and dubbed my library niche, "The Garret."

As we aged during the next eighteen years, I gradually convinced Emi to make improvements for our health and safety and to widen my own little space upstairs. New flooring downstairs, area rugs, and fresh, lighter-colored paint on the walls and woodwork brightened our living space, much to her eventual delight! A large dining room table and chairs, a new sofa and two comfortable easy chairs in the living room, a brand new queen bed in the extra bedroom, and the addition of a front concrete walkway made our guests more comfortable, too, and our home more accessible. As devoted partners, we shared all expenses equally. Each improvement was a challenge to Emi as I learned that change was difficult for her. In my mind, however, change has always been the only constant in life.

I even suggested improvements in the front, side, and back yards, making them more usable. Eventually, we cut back trees and brush, reclaimed land for a perennial flower garden, built a side yard patio and walkway with Pennsylvania blue stone, and began to create new, shared memories in our use of them. We became famous in the neighborhood for our patio picnics in the side yard behind our colorful, perennial flower garden. Neighbors walking by were invited on the spot to share our lunch or dinner, or just to sit a spell, enjoying a cool drink and visiting with us for as long as they wished. Another favorite event was our annual summer cookout with family, friends, and neighbors enjoying food and conversation at tables set up in the shade of the wide-spreading beech tree in the front yard.

One evening, many years later, Emi and I chanced to view a new series on television called *Hoarders*. "Boy, I'm glad I am not like those people," Emi announced proudly when the show ended, as she visually appreciated anew the gleaming hardwood, the clean and comfortable furniture, and the lack of serious clutter in the living room and dining room.

Amused, I turned toward her and smiled. "That's only because I won't let you be," I responded lovingly.

In the third month of my widowhood, I contacted my attorney and explained that Emi had died in late August 2012, and I cried a fresh flood of tears over the phone. Patiently and kindly, my attorney assured me that she would take a look at Emi's trust and will, and would get back with me. A week later she called. "Don't get rid of anything," she directed, "until after I send an appraiser. You are the sole beneficiary, but there will be a hefty state inheritance tax because you and Emi were not legally related."

Two weeks later during the visit of our close friend Hayden, the appraiser knocked at the front door. In his world of appraising and auctioneering, I am sure that the man who stood before me was honest and honorable, but every word he said to me that day became an irritation, as I ushered him into the living room and introduced my friend.

"Show me all her possessions," he demanded, "since you are no blood relative. Let's start right here." His auctioneer's eyes swept keenly over the antiques.

"We purchased most of this furniture together," I tried to explain.

"Well, which pieces did you buy together, then? You will only have to pay taxes on half," he insisted without a polite interval.

His ridiculous words and this whole intrusion were finally too much. I burst into tears. Clearly shaken at my response, the appraiser slipped into the dining room and phoned my attorney. After listening to his problem, my attorney directed him not to include any furniture or wall hangings in the appraisal. I collected myself once more and led this stranger through each room in the house, beginning in the basement and working our way up through the first and second floors. I cried quietly as he invaded my privacy, taking notes on all contents that belonged to my beloved Emi. Deeply concerned about me, my friend followed along behind, supporting me with his presence. When we reached my closed bedroom door at the top of the stairs, I had suffered enough. I refused to open the door. "There is nothing in my bedroom that belongs to her. We are finished here," I insisted.

After almost two hours, the invasive tour ended, and I hopefully wished the appraiser gone. Instead, he announced, "Now I need to go through all the rooms once more and take pictures of her belongings." It was too much! The tears flowed freely down my anguished face. Obvious to Hayden that I could not continue, he kindly volunteered to take the appraiser through each room again, and I gratefully nodded, unable to speak.

Many months later, the state of Indiana collected over twelve thousand dollars from me in inheritance taxes because Emi and I were not related. Yet married heterosexuals inherited everything and owed nothing at the death of a spouse. I sobbed aloud in the silent house as I wrote the check and mailed it to the state treasurer, sadly understanding how unequal I was in the land of the free, which Emi and I had always loved with our whole hearts. Three years later, in June 2015, same-sex marriages were nationally recognized by the Supreme Court as a right guaranteed by the Fourteenth Amendment, at long last correcting the injustice of senseless legal discrimination against gays and lesbians. Sadly, this ruling came too late for Emi and me.

Elizabeth Kidwell

Sixty days since I lost you,
And today an appraiser, with no search warrant,
Invaded
Every room of our home
Looking for your assets and taking pictures.

It seems that the State,
Though you left it nothing in your will,
Wants its inheritance money.
Told that I am not a blood relative,
I stand aside and have no
Rights.

No blood relative?
For twenty-five years
We lived as One,
A family,
Bone and flesh and breath
Together.
What outrageous injustice tells me
Otherwise?

Here in our home,
Every single thing tells a story about
Us,
Memories I treasure in the secret places of my heart:
Priceless.

Wounded Wings

        Do they not realize that I would give
        Everything
        Just to have you back?
        And yet, they took no picture of me
        Though I
        Completely
        Belonged to you.

Chapter 6
Soldier Girl

Eight months after we met, Emi asked me for my social security number. "Why?" I asked, instantly puzzled.

"Just trust me," she insisted. "I will explain everything to you later." I wrote the number down and handed it to her.

Two weeks later, after a glorious fall day spent hiking, birdwatching, and picnicking, Emi and I lay down side by side holding hands on the soft grass of a black walnut grove in Morgan-Monroe State Forest. For a while, we were surrounded by the comfortable silence that two people experience when they are securely in love. The forest was quiet except for the humming of bees and the distant call of a blue jay.

Emi squeezed my hand and began to speak. "Darling," she began in her sweet, gentle voice, "I have so much to tell you today. If we are going to continue to share our lives, there are important things you need to know about me."

Her strange words alarmed me, and my breath caught in my throat. "Is this why you needed my social security number?" I asked, fearful that our perfect life was about to come crashing down all around me.

"Yes, I had to have you cleared for security purposes and for permission to tell you certain things about me that no one else knows."

"How did I do?"

Emi gave my hand a loving squeeze. "You passed with flying colors!"

"All right then," I said, sounding braver than I actually felt, "go ahead."

"I am not just a retired school teacher," she confessed, her words strong and direct. "I also belong to an organization of the United States government that we call the Company. Our job is to collect military intelligence in support of our national defense."

For a moment I was stunned, speechless. A teacher who is also a spy? Who does that? Then I remembered that Emi had told me once that her paternal grandmother, Cordelia Hale, who died shortly after giving birth to her father, had been a distant relative of a young school teacher from Connecticut. He had been captured by the British during the American Revolution and hanged as a spy.

"You're a spy," I whispered, more statement than question. She nodded and smiled at me lovingly.

Then she continued, "During World War II, I wanted to join the Army and see combat, but women were forbidden to fight. So I was recruited by the Company, a different way of serving my country. They trained me well for every mission. I developed an excellent memory. I received expert training in military parachuting, in driving military vehicles, in sharp shooting, and in using other combat weapons. I was trained in hand to hand combat and learned to kill a person with my bare hands."

Emi took a deep breath and continued, "I was also given lessons in how to pleasure men and women sexually. I used sex to gain information and to infiltrate criminal organizations. During my missions all over the world, I obtained vital intelligence. A few missions involved killing the enemy," she explained sadly, her voice lowering slightly. "I have killed six people in my service to my country. Only one life do I regret taking. I also regret that six Marines sacrificed their lives to save mine when a mission went horribly wrong in Vietnam. I almost died afterwards, but they got me out. This memory haunts me."

"You are retired from teaching," I said. "Are you also retired from the Company?"

"Not yet," she answered solemnly, squeezing my hand.

My mind reeled and my heart sank. The more she spoke about her experiences, the sadder I became. I already loved her very much, but these stories were too hard to believe, preposterous, in fact. I began to think she was crazy, making this all up, using her vivid imagination. But why, I wondered. Was she lying to me? Why would she do that?

Now her words came pouring forth like a spring flood. Her great anguish inside forced the words out as she described the horrific events of many missions without ever once revealing their objectives or specific locations. The more she shared, the deeper my heart sank.

Nothing she is telling me can be true, I thought, silently trying to ward off her words when the horrifying mental pictures became too much for my peace loving mind.

After a long time, Emi grew silent. We both lay still afterwards, she recovering strength that the telling sapped from her, and I reeling from information now taking up a disquieting residence in my mind.

Finally, she spoke once more. "I suffer from PTSD," she continued with some effort. I take antidepressants, and the Army provides me with an excellent therapist, whom I see quite often. Nevertheless, I continue to have flashbacks and violent nightmares. That is why we can never sleep together at night. It would be too dangerous. If I would ever hurt you, I could never forgive myself. I love you so much." At those words she took me in her arms and held me close for a long time.

Hours later, as she drove home, neither of us talked. I was crushed by the possibility that I might have to let this wonderful woman go. Just the thought made me cry inside. Emi seemed lost in her own thoughts, possibly wondering what effect her disclosures were having on me. Arriving at her house in the late afternoon, we unloaded the car. I was spent. I needed to process all that had occurred, so I climbed the stairs to the guest room, where I spent most weekends, and lay down on the bed, mentally and emotionally exhausted. I assumed that Emi was resting, too. It was eerily quiet downstairs. Then, I heard her voice calling up to me, "Ellie, could you come down here, please?"

I found her in her bedroom. When I entered, I saw a large, red box lying prominently on her bed, my name printed in black letters on the lid. She smiled at me warmly. "I want to show you something," she said in a voice so incredibly soft, that I could just detect a mixture of sadness and anticipation.

Emi opened the box and began to take out what appeared to be dark blue jewelry boxes edged in gold. Three smaller ones were embossed with the words, "Purple Heart," and eight larger ones said "United States of America," all in gold lettering. One by one she took them reverently out of the box and handed them to me. "They awarded me these for my service," she explained, her sweet face registering pain, but her strong voice sounding like pride.

What treasure I held in my hands! Each case contained a large service medal, a smaller one, a ribbon bar, and a matching lacquered pin. I had never seen such awards in my life. They were beautiful and impressive, and Emi explained what each medal meant. There were more medals in smaller, plain jewelry boxes also, so many, that I lost count. When she finished sharing her awards with me, she packed them back in the red box and placed it under her bed. Then she turned to face me. She pulled me to her and hugged me tight. "When I die," she announced, placing her sweet face next to mine, "they will all be yours."

I never wanted to look at her medals again because I understood that when I had to, she would be gone. I knew where they were, and my mind was at ease. I gradually came to believe that she was telling the truth, and my respect for her grew each day as well as my love.

One afternoon several years later, I returned home from school to find Emi sitting at the dining room table, holding a wooden 8 by 10 inch glass-fronted display frame. Inside the case she had arranged and mounted all of her small medals. "What are you doing?" I asked curiously.

"Well, I had a therapy session this morning out at the fort," she explained, "and Linda decided that I need to take more pride in my service. She suggested that I display my medals so that I view them each day. I am going to hang them on my bedroom wall, so only you and I will see them." That is where they stayed for many years. When she finally took them down, I didn't notice. I was too busy working full time at school, and at home, I was taking on more and more responsibilities as Emi aged.

Four months before Emi died, I took her to the emergency department at St. Vincent's Hospital for a serious bladder infection. During her second night in the hospital, she suffered a reaction to her antibiotic and vomited in her sleep in the middle of the night. It was not discovered until early morning, and by that time, the damage was done. Her nurse called me immediately and told me to come quickly. Emi was rushed to ICU, where she almost died from aspiration pneumonia. When I arrived at the hospital, Emi was very sick and incoherent, but gradually over the next two days in intensive care, her strong love for me and her even stronger will to live allowed her to recover. By the time she was released from the hospital ten days later, she was suffering from congestive heart failure and was transferred to a rehabilitation center five minutes from our house in order to allow her to regain enough strength to return home and for me to regain enough energy to continue caring for her.

During her absence, I used the opportunity to buy her a new lower bed, foundation, and mattress so that she could climb in and out of bed more easily. As I dismantled her mother's tall, wooden, antique bed, I discovered that the red box underneath was missing. Later, I found the box in the basement, completely empty. I felt a combination of confusion and sadness. Had she changed her mind about the medals? The day I brought Emi home from rehab, I ushered her into her bedroom to try out her new bed. Then I told her, "I found the red box in the basement empty. Where are the medals that I am supposed to get if you die before I do?"

"Oh," she explained as she looked at me and smiled, "my attorney has them at his office. He will give them to you after I die."

Puzzled, I smiled back at her and said, "All right, but that will be a long time from now." I was overjoyed to have her home again, but because she was still weak, the questions I really wanted answered, forever remained unspoken.

Wounded Wings

You were the ultimate soldier:
A woman
Without a uniform,
Unsuspected,
Putting life and spirit on hold
To save others, people unknown to you,
From dark strangers
And risking your peace for duty and freedom.

Often you were dropped behind enemy lines,
Parachuting
Your bold heart and body into dangerous worlds,
The closest you ever came to fear,
My brave, beloved heroine.

The lives you had to take
Took life from you,
And every death you lived
A thousand times
In your fevered dreams,
Crying out in horror
As I held you close.

Over and over, I reminded you
In soft whispers
That our love was your reality,
Not the combat buried,
And when you recovered

To find only comfort and warmth
In my arms,
You lay down your weapons and
Surrendered
To me.

Chapter 7
Grappled

Once Emi and I set our love in motion, we never looked back. Ever forward, deeper and deeper, our loving relationship grew, and we began to explore our inner and outer worlds regularly.

The language of our shared love was touch, intimacy. While we spoke of love every day, we really didn't need to. A tender glance, a bright smile, a soft moan, a gentle touch spoke eloquently of the wonder of our togetherness more than any words could. Making love was priority time, and we gave our best selves to each other over and over. Often, our loving was so beautiful and intense that I cried. Other times, we laughed joyously, and I was filled with wonder that two people could ever be this close. We always seemed to bring out the best in each other. I know that our love was so precious to Emi because when the love of her life died after thirty years together, she never expected to find another. I was her happy surprise! Emi expressed her wonder in a short note to me. "It is such joy to have you come and walk into my awaiting arms as you have truly walked into my heart and my very life. So much I want to share with you, places, events, thoughts, dreams, my very life, yes, yes, and yes again! Beth always quoted, '…the last for which the first was made.' Yes, our love is that for which the 'first' was made! Because of you, each day will be rich. I shall continue in completeness and gain purpose."

The result of our first years of intense closeness was this: we were completely one in body, soul, heart, and mind, never to be separated again. I was grappled to her. Oh, Emi took trips alone, especially to Elderhostels, and I missed her completely, but her love was always such a palpable presence to me, that even in her absence, she was never really gone. I often traveled to visit my parents, siblings and friends in California, over 2,000 miles away, and Emi encouraged it. She firmly believed that our separate trips enhanced our relationship, and our homecomings were always memorable! We shared deeply the joys experienced and the insights learned while we were apart, and our short absences from each other only served to tighten and strengthen our bond and to grow our love. Never a day passed, no matter where we were, together or apart, that we did not speak. We ended every conversation the same way that we ended every day, with the words, "I love you." Three squeezes while holding hands was a secret code we shared, so that we could say "I love you" even when we could not speak, like in the movies or in a crowd! We knew in the depths of our being that the words were true because our daily interaction spoke eloquently of our love, respect, and joy for each other without even saying a word.

Emi and I also shared a great love of adventure. We began every trip by singing, "We're going on an adventure to see what we can see," set to the tune of "The Bear Went over the Mountain." When I was a child, vacations with my family always included lots of singing on the road, often with radio accompaniment. Emi eagerly adopted this tradition.

Early on, we purchased a book titled, *Off the Beaten Path*, and it became a sort of bible for us when we traveled in the United States. One of our favorite places in the book was Little Girl's Point on Lake Superior near Ironwood, Michigan, on the upper peninsula. The beach there consisted of millions of multi-colored rounded stones worn smooth by Superior's waves. The rocks at the shoreline were tiny, but they gradually increased in size the farther we walked away from the lakeshore. Rock hounds, both of us, we filled a wooden box with stones of different sizes and colors, and no one was present to stop us! While there, we learned that Little Girl's Point got its name from a Chippewa Indian legend, and this knowledge enriched our visit even more.

Another out-of-the-way attraction in the book was memorable to us for an entirely different reason. On a later trip to Minnesota, Emi and I decided to visit Indian Mounds Park near West Bend, Wisconsin, to view eighteen historical mounds in a peaceful, wooded area. When we pulled into the small parking lot, a black sedan with heavily-tinted windows was pulling out. Otherwise, the lot was deserted. Happily, we parked our Volkswagen, slathered ourselves with mosquito repellent, locked the car, and headed toward the heavily-wooded trail, eager to learn about the mounds. We would have this beautiful location all to ourselves! However, as we entered the shaded woodland, out of the corner of my eye, I noticed that the same black car was slowly and mysteriously returning to the parking area. At first, I didn't say anything to Emi because I didn't want to alarm her. As we strolled along, her attention was directed to the mounds and the interpretive information at each stop, but nervously, I kept glancing back down the trail. Sure enough, a tall man who appeared to be in his thirties, emerged from the shadows and onto the trail. It was apparent that he was following us because he was not looking at the mounds. He stayed about fifty yards back as we walked along, his wide, menacing eyes clearly focused on us, his progress matching ours.

"Emi," I said quietly, "I think we're in trouble. Look behind us." Without a word, she glanced back, took my hand, squeezed it lovingly three times, and together we walked on to the next mound. This time we both looked back, and there he was, watching us intently! I felt the hair at the back of my neck rise up. Instinctively, I bent down and grabbed a club-sized fallen tree branch.

It was then that Emi and I quickened our pace, the Indian mounds completely abandoned in our alarm. My heart pounded frantically inside my chest as my adrenaline rose and my body went into fight or flight mode. I was truly frightened for us both, though Emi seemed deadly calm. I knew then clearly that I would seriously hurt this man before I would let him harm Emi. I turned back, brandishing the club and staring directly at the man in warning. By nature a gentle, nonviolent person, I was alarmed by my ferocity and resolve. Breaking into the clearing, Emi and I hurried to our car. Only when she was safely inside, did I throw down my club and climb in too, locking the doors. I backed up the car and pulled behind the man's vehicle as Emi wrote down the license plate number. Just then, the ominous stranger emerged from the trees, saw what we were doing, and turned tail, sprinting back into the woods. As we drove away, I wondered if he even sensed just how close he had come to dying.

Emi loved life and everything it had to offer just like I did. Sharing our life with other people, animals, birds, oceans, lakes, rivers, mountains, and even the sky made us rich beyond imagining. Every five years or so, we made it a point to board a sailing vessel in order to go whale watching. We wanted to see for ourselves if earth's largest mammal was still doing well in our oceans. Sometimes we embarked from the Atlantic coast, other times from the Pacific. It didn't matter because the oceans were interconnected, just like we were.

I never met anyone who loved her time on this earth more than Emi. As she aged, her thirst for knowledge never wavered. While I worked, Emi spent much of her time learning. She took art classes at the Indianapolis Museum of Art, and her masterpieces adorned the walls of my bedroom. She signed up for a course in Chinese cuisine and surprised me with delicious dinners once a week. "This is what we learned in class today," she would announce proudly, serving up flavorful, steaming Asian food. During the day she also audited classes at Butler University, her Alma Mater, and in the evening she would always share with me the interesting information she had heard so that I could learn, too. When she realized how important my Native American heritage meant to me, she signed us up for an evening class at Butler featuring Native American spirituality and beliefs. Both the information and the lovely Native American woman who taught the class enriched our lives with fresh understanding and a new friendship. When Emi could no longer drive at night, I would take her to Mini-Medical School at Riley Hospital auditorium, sponsored by Indiana University School of Medicine. Once a week for years, she absorbed the wonders of modern medicine. For each course completed, she received a certificate. She acquired so many of them that eventually I addressed her as "Mini-Doc Emi."

The day before Emi died, a young doctor called me out into the hallway. "She is not responding to the second antibiotic," he explained sadly. The aspiration pneumonia was back as a result of her stroke, but this time her weakened body was not able to fight it off. With her entire right side paralyzed, the prognosis was grim. "There is nothing more we can do," he concluded. "It is time to call Hospice."

"Have you told her yet?" I asked.

The doctor's eyes widened at my words. "Well no," he responded, as if informing people that they were dying was not part of his job description.

"I'll tell her," I said, sounding braver than I really was. The doctor's face relaxed and he looked grateful.

Informing my Beloved that the life she loved so fiercely would soon come to an end was the hardest and the saddest responsibility I have ever performed. I was holding Emi's left hand, and as she listened, she became very quiet, weighing my words. Thankfully, she was in no pain yet. I explained to her that Hospice had been called and would meet with us later. When the social worker from Hospice arrived, we arranged to have Emi transported to the nursing facility adjacent to the rehab center, very close to home. An ambulance would come for her in the morning. But this was one planned trip that Emi never made. She had another, more important journey on her mind.

At 6:00 the next morning, she took a turn for the worst. Since she had a DNR in place, all IV's had been removed the previous day. When it was obvious that Emi was in distress, the nurse asked my permission to start an IV for pain medication. "I know she is in pain," she explained, "but she is trying to act brave."

"It's no act," I responded. "She is brave. Please, I want her to be comfortable, and I do not want her to suffer," I said as I agreed to intravenous pain medication. "She is allergic to morphine," I added. I held Emi and our eyes locked together in love and pain as a special nurse arrived and inserted an IV needle using a small ultrasound machine to guide her. When the first dose of Delaudid was finally administered, Emi slipped into a peaceful sleep. For the next three hours I sat next to her holding her left hand, and out of habit, I squeezed her hand gently three times to let her know that I was present and that I loved her. At 9:00 a.m. I once again squeezed Emi's hand reassuring her of my presence and love. Immediately came her response: three firm squeezes. Those were the last three words that Emi ever said to me. During the next eleven hours, Emi and I made the longest journey of our lives, but this time, there was no way I could protect her.

Wounded Wings

From your very beginning
You seized life in both hands
And held on tightly to the thrill

Of riding proudly on this earth,
Face to the wind, offering resistance
To anything that dared to hold you back.

And when your life had slowed
Enough for me to climb aboard,
You lay hold of me like a whirlwind,

Clasped me closely to your heart,
Soaring me to heights and depths
I thought unattainable in this world.

From that moment, backward glance, never.
Dashing forward at breakneck speed,
Grabbing and gripping each miracle

As if it were our last, mastering minutes,
Seizing seconds, panting for breath.
You, greedy for living, enfolded me safe.

Even as you aged, speed never wavered,
Outracing years, daring time to catch you
In your sprint to the finish line, heedless.

Only when you lay breathless could
Death loosen your grip. Yet, here I am,
Flying toward infinity, still bound to you

Chapter 8
Suicide Hill

Winter was always a joyous time for Emi and me. We loved the outdoors, and even ice and snow failed to concern us. An only child, Emi had been incredibly close to her mother, and one of the ways we honored her memory was to continue a sweet tradition that she had begun when Emi was a little girl. Her mother Marie believed that her family should have a picnic every month of the year. Now that her parents were gone and I was her family, I agreed with Emi that we should carry on this important practice. So we picnicked every month for the next twenty-five years, and no matter where we ate, the ritual was always the same. We raised our glasses and toasted her mom, "To Marie, the founder of the feast!" And Emi would always add, glancing skyward, "Thanks, Mom!"

The weather was no obstacle to our monthly picnics. We packed our lunch and ate it outside, in any weather, wherever we happened to be traveling. We had picnics in almost every state, including Alaska! When we were home in Indianapolis, we would hold picnics either at Eagle Creek City Park or at Fort Harrison State Park, and often, other people were invited.

One January, the snow, the ice, and the bone-numbing cold had socked in for a solid month with no sign of a thaw. Emi and I had waited all month for the weather to break, but now with only one day left, we faced possibly the coldest picnic we had ever shared. The next day in preparation, with the local temperature at minus 30 degrees, Emi and I donned our long underwear, several layers of pullover shirts and sweaters, flannel-lined jeans, two pairs of wool socks, heavily lined snow boots, down jackets, neck mufflers, two pairs of gloves, ear muffs, and heavy knitted caps. In our food bag we packed thermoses of hot tea and hot soup, crackers, ham and cheese sandwiches, and apples.

When Emi and I arrived at Eagle Creek Park, the roads were cleared, but everything else was covered with at least eight inches of icy snow. We drove to the skating pond because we knew that there was always a picnic table overlooking it, and we could park very close. The park was deserted except for us, but a tradition is a tradition, and we trudged carefully up the low rise to the table, clearing it and the benches with our gloved hands and the car hand broom. We spread dry, thick towels on the benches and used another as a tablecloth before sitting down.

Suffice it to say that this was the coldest and shortest picnic on record! The wind chill of icy-cold air knifed into our lungs. The soup and the tea warmed us slightly, and as we raised our plastic mugs in salute to Marie, Emi broke tradition and added a special message to her mother, "I hope you appreciate this!"

As teachers, one thing Emi and I appreciated more than most people was a snow day! Emi had purchased a blue, plastic two-person toboggan for use on Suicide Hill at Butler University, and she was just waiting for a chance to use it! Then, on a Sunday evening, just a few weeks following our freezing picnic, Indianapolis was bombarded with even more winter weather, a sleet and snow storm that dumped six more inches of slushy snow and ice on the city. It was followed by a night of sub-freezing temperatures, which turned the slush into rock-hard ice! By morning, school was cancelled all over the city.

At breakfast, a beaming Emi, hardly able to contain her joy over a free day with me, announced, "Let's go sledding on Suicide Hill!" She was so excited and happy that I didn't have the heart to say no to her or to caution her about the inherent dangers. We bundled up once again, put the plastic toboggan into the backseat, and drove the six blocks to the double-sloped hill known to everyone in the neighborhood as Suicide.

Usually when there is snow followed by a snow day, Suicide Hill is crowded with families enjoying a chance to sled. So it should have been a warning to us when we arrived to find the glass-slick hill deserted, except for two college-aged young men taking turns sliding down the hill, with both feet crammed into a white, five-gallon painter's bucket while holding onto the handle! We paused a few minutes to observe the fools. I immediately voiced my misgivings, but Emi was undaunted as she pulled the nylon rope of our light toboggan behind her and trudged carefully to the top of the hill. For our first run, my beloved daredevil naturally chose the front, and I happily settled in behind her just in case I had to bury my head in her back to avoid facing my fear. We used our feet like a turtle's to inch forward to the edge of the hill. Then suddenly, we were off!

Oh, in my childhood I had careened down snowy winter slopes in the Sierra-Nevada with my siblings and cousins at the back of a fourteen-man toboggan, but this ride with Emi was even more exhilarating! Perhaps, it was because I was hugging my Emi and flying by pure love. I don't know, but that ride felt like shooting down the steep hill on an ice rocket, so fast that I could not catch my breath! Finally, we slicked down the hill and out across the flat ice, wind and friction slowing us down and stopping us just short of the chain-link fence that enclosed the hill.

"Wow! That was wonderful!" Emi cheered, totally thrilled as she jumped up and down. "Let's go again! Only this time, go to the car and get that wool blanket so we can sit on it. I'll pull the toboggan back up the hill. Meet me at the top."

"All right," I agreed, tramping over the crunchy ice, careful not to slip, "but make sure you walk straight up the track we made coming down. There are some ridges of ice at the base of the hill." I pointed to some tire tracks made by a large, heavy vehicle in the slush, which had wickedly hardened overnight into eight-inch ice ridges. If we hit those at a high speed, I realized, they could cause our tiny toboggan to go airborne. Concerned, I stamped on several of the ice ridges in an attempt to flatten them. "Let's just make sure we hit this same chute," I cautioned.

Five minutes later, Emi and I met again at the top of the icy hill. I folded the blanket to fit into the sled's trough, and we settled down more comfortably into the same positions, kicking off. The ride down Suicide was as smooth and swift as before, but just before we arrived at the bottom, I peeked over Emi's shoulder and realized that we were no longer in our original chute. Thick, solid ice ridges loomed ahead of us, and I realized instantly that at the speed we were traveling, we were doomed! I grabbed Emi even tighter, wrapping my arms and legs around her like protective packaging.

As we smacked the ice ridge hard, our toboggan tipped to the right, slightly airborne, and I took the force of the blow as my head, right shoulder, and arm slammed against the ice. I flew off the sled still holding Emi, but came to rest without her, spread-eagled on the cold ice, stars twinkling above me like you see in cartoons! Where was she? How was she?

Then, Emi was standing over me, seemingly unhurt. "Get up!" she commanded excitedly, obviously ready for another run, her cheeks and nose red from the cold.

Try as I might, I realized that I could not move my right arm. Something was weighing it down. "Is there something on my right arm?" I asked, grimacing in pain.

"Just the blanket."

"Could you take it off, please?" When Emi removed the blanket, I slowly and painfully pulled my arm closer to my body. "It feels warm and sticky inside my sleeve," I explained, and for the first time, Emi studied me, seriously concerned. "My head hurts, too," I said, "but I think my ear muffs saved me."

"Let's go home and check it out," she insisted, gathering the blanket and grabbing the rope to the sled. Slowly we climbed the hill, heading for her car. She opened the passenger door for me and closed it after me once I was inside. Throwing the blanket and the toboggan into the backseat, she drove the short distance home. Once inside the house, Emi helped me remove my jacket and several layers of sweaters and long-sleeved tops, down to my short-sleeved T-shirt. At each layer, we looked for blood but didn't find any. Finally, my arm was exposed, swollen at the elbow to almost twice its normal size. "I'm taking you to the emergency department," Emi declared, her eyes registering alarm. "You need an X-ray. There might be something broken inside, and you need your head examined also." This was a switch, Emi driving me to the emergency department! It was usually the other way around. As for the head examination, that should have occurred before I climbed on the sled!

At the hospital I was ushered into a cubicle, and I removed my down jacket. "Whoa!" the nurse exclaimed in awe. "What a massive hematoma!"

Elizabeth Kidwell

After an X-ray revealed no broken bones, the ER doctor recommended that I take the next two days off school to rest for my slight concussion, keep my arm elevated in the provided sling, and avoid driving my car for at least a week. He concluded our visit by asking, "So you slipped on the ice, huh?"

"Oh, no!" Emi exclaimed, pride flashing in her eyes. "We wiped out while sledding down Suicide Hill!" The doctor's eyes registered surprise, but the wide-eyed look he gave us clearly communicated his suspicion that senile dementia had apparently arrived early for Emi and me, and we both needed our heads examined!

For the rest of the week, Emi drove me to and from school, but wisely, I did not take any days off. As I walked into the school building on Tuesday morning, my principal was standing outside her office to greet her teachers and to ask how we enjoyed our free day. Seeing me with my right arm in a sling, she shook her head, clearly amused. Her only comment as I passed was, "You were with Emi yesterday, weren't you?" I smiled at her and nodded.

"And for always," I whispered softly to myself as I continued happily down the hallway to my classroom.

Wounded Wings

Snow day!
Music to our minds,
Two teachers
Who thought of nothing
But a free day together
Braving bitter cold
For the sheer joy
Of riding the ice
Down Suicide Hill
On a two-women toboggan,
The thrill of flying
And hot chocolate
Adding to the promise
Of the day.
The sheer downhill speed
Glorious!
Frosty wind
Skinning our faces,
Plunging headlong
Down the glass-ice slope
For the daring excitement
Of pure acceleration!

Elizabeth Kidwell

Another trudge up the hill
And then our rocket sled
Outracing the wind,
Reckless pursuit of cold freedom
Until a ridge of ice loomed ahead
And doomed our ride
To airborne flight.

Pressing you against me, safe,
Crashing into rock-hard ice
With arm and head,
Little saved me from the stars.
You unhurt. Thankfully,
I made a good cushion.

Emergency room diagnosis:
Massive hematoma and
Slight concussion,
But the pain was nothing
Compared to the absolute joy
Of holding you close
As we broke the love barrier!

Wounded Wings

Chapter 9
Pumpkin

Emi's favorite month was October. Everything about this month was perfect as far as she was concerned. She was born on the seventh; her beloved mother was born on the fourteenth. That alone was enough to make it sacred! Halloween was always a happy holiday for her. From childhood she had loved the costumes, the kids, the candy, the treats, the tricks, and the whole idea of going from house to house at night incognito, begging and scaring people! Every Halloween, we filled up sacks of goodies to distribute to the neighborhood children who knocked at our door, and we invited them and their parents inside for a short chat, so we could admire their little witches and pirates! Then the kids could take as much candy as their parents would allow.

When it came to her birthday, Emi celebrated during the whole month! If her friends were not taking her out to lunch, we were attending fall fish fries and festivals every weekend like the Feast of the Hunter's Moon in Lafayette or the Covered Bridge Festival in Parke County. We also joined thousands of our fellow Hoosiers and drove to Nashville, Indiana, and Brown County State Park to admire all the color. Best of all, the decorations were free! October in Indiana was peak month for fall foliage, and the beauty we cherished each year could never be topped. So the month-long October celebration tradition was easy for me to adopt.

In fact, Emi's enthusiasm for October gave me a brilliant idea. Emi's mother died when she was 69, and her father died when he was 72. An only child, Emi was always trying to prepare me for the chance that she might expire while she was relatively young. I would have none of it. So I hatched a plan. "On your sixty-fifth birthday," I announced one day, "I will give you a blowout birthday open house and invite all of your friends!"

Emi grinned as wide as a jack-o'-lantern's smile! "You mean it?" she asked, her soft brown eyes glowing brightly with anticipatory excitement. There was nothing she loved more than being the center of attention.

"Absolutely!" I exclaimed. "In fact, if you enjoy it, I will repeat the open house birthday party every five years for as long as you live!" Well, Emi's life from that point on became a kind of contest. She happily counted down the years to the next birthday bash!

Her sixty-fifth birthday party was a hit, not only with Emi, but also with all her friends! Everyone thought it was a wonderful idea and flocked to our door to visit with and pay homage to the queen of October! Beautiful people, including many teachers who had taught with Emi, enjoyed a catered feast and the chance to visit with each other. All day long, her friends kept up a steady stream of visits until early evening. After the last guests said their goodbyes, Emi took me into her arms and kissed me warmly. "I loved every minute of my open house," she announced. "Thank you so much! It was the best gift you could ever give me."

"Well," I responded happily, believing in my heart that my plan was off to a great start, "play your cards right, and you can have another one in five years for your seventieth!"

The only problem I had not foreseen was that Emi kept making new friends, so that the five-year parties grew larger and larger! After attending the funeral of two friends her age, Emi adopted a new policy. Tired of losing good friends and worried about running out of them, she decided to begin making younger friends! In fact, "Make younger friends" became her new motto, and subsequently her advice to me.

As I had hoped, Emi looked forward to living a long time to enjoy her five-year parties! She took better care of herself, had regular medical checkups, took her medicine, ate the healthful meals I prepared, and lived life to the fullest between each celebration. Happily and proudly, she counted down the years! I knew those open houses stayed on her mind because as we neared the next one, Emi would inform me, "Only one more year until my party!" My plan was working!

Elizabeth Kidwell

For Emi's seventieth birthday, friends flocked in from neighboring states, and we put close friends up at our house. The upside was that we had more people to help us prepare the feast; the work was cut in half, and Emi got longer visits! We began to photograph all of Emi's friends who attended the open house that year, especially the people who came from Missouri, New Jersey, and Florida. It was a good practice because another friend died before the next party and a few others became too old to travel again in five years, but Emi had lovely photos and precious memories to cherish. In between the five-year parties, Emi, who never knew a stranger, continued to make new and younger friends, so we never ran out of guests! For me, that meant that I had to save more money to feed them!

By Emi's seventy-fifth birthday bash, the party spilled out into the front yard under the shade of the spreading beech tree, which Emi had planted when she retired at sixty! There, we set up additional decorated tables and chairs. Because it was a milestone birthday, we also began serving champagne! Appreciatively, Emi's guests raised their glasses to her over and over! Many friends may have been concerned that Emi might not make it to eighty, so they arrived and celebrated at this one. The invitations that always preceded the celebrations explained that no presents were necessary. "Your very presence is a gift," each invitation explained. Every guest was indeed a gift and a blessing to Emi, and whether they understood it or not, their visits added years to Emi's life. She visibly "lit up" when each friend arrived like a surprise! Many people were friends she had not seen in years, and some guests were people even I had never met. It was beautiful that our guests stayed for a period of time, visited with Emi and each other, enjoyed food and drink, and then took their leave. Others arrived for lunch and left after dinner when the party was over. Still other friends lingered until after dark, and a few stayed overnight. No matter. We loved them all and were thrilled to see them. By the time the open house ended, Emi was exhausted but still riding high from all the love and good wishes. I had never seen her more elated!

By her eightieth birthday, Emi's party had become a neighborhood event as well. All the neighbors who knew us stopped by with their good wishes, laden with food, gifts, and flowers, and even neighbors who were just walking by were persuaded to join us just to celebrate life! A friend and neighbor at the end of the block, who had known Emi for seventy years, could not attend because at 103 years old, she was too feeble, but sweetly and thoughtfully, she sent her seventy-five year old daughter as her stand-in, bearing a box of expensive chocolates!

Former students of Emi's joined us that year as well. The few who had been formally invited passed the word around to other former classmates. These young and middle-aged people gathered around her in the living room, sitting happily at Emi's feet to share with her how their lives had unfolded and to thank her for being such a great influence in their lives. They explained to her what a special role model she had been, how the biology unit on birds and subsequent birding field trips had enriched their lives and had turned them into lifelong birdwatchers, a practice they were now sharing with their children. Emi listened with joy! She understood that so few teachers were privileged to learn how their students' lives were influenced by what they taught, and she was grateful to receive this gift. Emi was also overjoyed to learn how accomplished her students had become and how happy their lives had become. Best of all, her students hugged her warmly, assuring her of their love, respect, and gratitude.

For her eighty-fifth birthday open house, Emi's long-time friend Thom drove over from St. Louis with a special cake that his wife had baked and which he had personally decorated. In totally edible frosting, Thom had created a work of art. It was a phenomenal reproduction of the famous painting of *Napoleon Crossing the Alps* by French artist Jacques-Louis David, depicting the emperor rearing up astride his noble horse! Emi was delighted and amazed, as were all her guests, who took photo after photo of this magnificent masterpiece. It was such a lovely cake that it almost went uneaten until the end of the day when Emi ceremoniously cut a piece and discovered that the cake was as delicious as it was beautiful. Once that happened, Napoleon and his horse didn't stand a chance. They met a second Waterloo!

Emi never celebrated her ninetieth birthday, at least not here. She died at the age of eighty-seven, but she had lived longer than any other member of her family! My plan had worked, but not to my complete satisfaction. At no matter at what age she died, it would have been too soon for me. I loved that woman with all my being. In the directives she left me in the event of her death, she expressed the wish that she would be remembered at a memorial open house in her home just like her five-year parties! Two of our close friends encouraged me to hold the memorial celebration of her life on what would have been Emi's eighty-eighth birthday, just forty-one days after her death, and I agreed because I had promised her. I know that Emi wanted this open house so that our friends could be there to console me, but I just wasn't up for a party. The pain of my grief was still just as raw as the day she died, and I wanted to grieve privately. It took all of my courage and self-control not to cry. If my sister Louise had not returned to Indiana the week before the memorial, I doubt if it would have taken place at all. Lovingly, she planned the tasteful decorations and prepared the delicious food, and several of my friends arrived early to help her. I did try to do my part. Louise would give me a job, and zombie-like, I would complete it and then ask for another. Other than that, I was useless and sad.

Two hours into the memorial, when most of the guests had arrived and eaten, we all gathered in the living room. Scott, a gay minister, one of Emi's former biology students and lab assistants, invited her friends to share their favorite memories of Emi, and eagerly they did so. I sat silently in an easy chair, hearing many stories I had never known. I also listened as friend after friend described what a wonderful person Emi was.

Finally, it was the minister's turn to speak and as he did, I realized that Emi had one last trick to play on me. "Several years ago," he began, "Emi called me and we met for lunch. During our meal, she came out to me and told me that she was a lesbian."

Well, you could have heard a pin drop as over forty people collectively stopped breathing! Emi and I had never come out to any family, friends, or neighbors because, as teachers, we had wanted to keep our jobs, and Emi grew up in an era where people just didn't share these matters and for good reason. At Scott's words, I wavered between jumping up and exclaiming "I didn't know that!" to break the tension and to get a laugh, or sinking completely through the seat cushion to disappear! What I did do was to sit there dignified and proud as everyone in the room slowly began to realize that I had lost so much more than my best friend.

Nothing more was said, and within a half hour, guests began to leave, some without even telling me goodbye and others without looking me in the eyes, as if they were ashamed of me, or maybe because they were ashamed of themselves. I figured that I had lost a good number of friends that day just by being who I was, and indeed, some of these people I never saw again. I was relieved that Emi was not here to see it. However, it didn't take me long to realize that a great deal of freedom and relief comes from being out to friends and family, and I decided that maybe this revelation was a special gift from Emi. She had never enjoyed this complete freedom, but she wanted me to have it!

Over the succeeding months, I had many meaningful talks with family, friends, and neighbors, sharing with them my pain of loss. It also gave me joy to express to them how special and important Emi, my loving partner, had been in my life. My sister Louise shared with me that she had figured it out long ago, and that our parents, who knew Emi, had also understood and accepted it. Later, when I visited my sister Kathleen in Illinois, I came out to her. She expressed her awareness bluntly, "No surprise to me!" she exclaimed. "I always knew you two were in love whenever you came to visit. Every time Emi looked at you, I saw pure love in her eyes. There was no mistaking that!" Then, she hugged me, and I, true to form, burst into tears.

Elizabeth Kidwell

I called you my sweet-faced pumpkin,
Punk for short.
Your perfectly round head, filled with enough ideas
To light a thousand lamps, was surpassed solely
By the glowing grin that animated your face
And set my heart on fire whenever you
Turned that smile on me.

Every day of my life with you was Halloween.
You tricked and treated me repeatedly
With adventure and surprise and life,
And each evening I entered the front door,
Porch light blazing,
As if you were expecting a thousand beggars
Instead of just one weary impostor
With palms extended for a handout.

What you gave me, poured into
My panhandling heart
From the treasures of your loving care
Was sweetness beyond imagining!
You filled me over and over each day
With such satisfying life, sugary love,
That I never had to appear at another house
To ask for blessings. They were all right here.

Chapter 10
Fallen

Before Emi entered her eighties, falling became a problem and a danger. If I was home, I would hear a soft thud followed by Emi's standard exclamation, "Oh, damn!" In her sixties, she had developed a condition called orthostatic hypotension. What it meant was that if she was sitting for a long period of time and rose from her chair too quickly, her blood pressure would plummet and so would she! She fainted and fell hard. We never knew when it would occur, but the concept of rising slowly was lost on Emi, who had spent her entire life leaping up, always eager to be on the go. It wasn't that she didn't recognize the danger of rising quickly; she just forgot.

Other physical conditions caused her to fall as well. Emi had developed neuropathy in her feet and legs during her seventies, despite the fact that she was never diabetic. The disorder caused her pain and numbness, so that she had to take heavy doses of a medication called Neurontin daily. Before she was diagnosed, wearing shoes was a problem. She began to buy a new pair of shoes each month, desperate to find footwear that would not cause her discomfort. She never succeeded until we attended a Native American pow-wow, and she discovered that she could tolerate moccasins. From then on, Emi tread gently on Mother Earth. Gradually, I noticed however, that Emi began to stay home more; she drove less, and saddest of all, she could no longer participate in birdwatching hikes because her feet became numb and painful when she walked, and moccasins could not protect her feet when she stepped on rocks.

A third condition that caused Emi to fall often was more subtle to detect, but gradually I discovered from observation that whenever Emi stepped backwards, she would lose her balance and fall. Convincing her that stepping backward was a danger to her took some doing but eventually Emi recognized the problem for what it was and tried very hard to avoid it.

When I arrived home from school one early spring afternoon, Emi was all smiles, as if she had just won the lottery! "Look!" she exclaimed happily, pointing to a turquoise-colored contraption sitting in the middle of the living room floor. "I drove up to Wheel Chairs and More today and bought this outdoor walker." Emi pointed out all its special features: a huge basket that fastened in front to hold bird books, binoculars, water bottles, or just about anything. "You can put your stuff in this basket too," she offered generously. The walker sat on four, equally-sized hard rubber wheels, making it easy to push and maneuver over rugged terrain. It had handle bars with attached hand brakes for sudden stops. Best of all, it sported a wide seat for resting when walking became too painful. It also folded up for easy storage in the car. After she had explained all the features, I had to admit that it was a beauty. Emi was beaming!

"I think we should take her out for a trial run this Saturday at Eagle Creek Park," I suggested, delighted to see that youthful enthusiasm return to her face once more. The outdoor walker proved to be a blessing. For two more years Emi was able to go places and do things she loved, either alone or with me, because of her "wonder walker." Eventually, however, she slowed down again as the walker became too heavy for her to lift into her car.

One Saturday morning at breakfast, I took Emi's hand in mine and gazed into her soft brown eyes. "Let's go to Wheel Chairs and More this morning," I suggested. "I think it is time to get a collapsible wheelchair that will enable us to continue our journeys together so you won't miss a minute." I hoped that she would be excited about the idea, but she was less than pleased at first, as if the words "wheelchair" and "feeble" were synonymous.

Reluctantly, Emi accompanied me to the store. When we entered, I explained to the manager that we were looking for a rugged, collapsible wheelchair that would be suitable for indoor or outdoor use, one that would fit easily into my car. Without hesitation, he showed us a black, lightweight model that had all of the features we were looking for. Emi sat in it and pronounced it comfortable. The manager demonstrated how easily it collapsed and opened again. He showed us how the footrests detached and reattached. Finally, we wheeled the chair outside for the automobile fit test. Hand to glove! Sold! Emi, ever practical yet fashion conscious, chose a bright red wheelchair pack accessory to hold our gear. We were on our way home in no time.

After pulling into the driveway, I lifted the wheelchair out of my VW Jetta wagon, opened it, and attached the footrests. "Let's go for a spin in the neighborhood," I suggested. Reluctantly, Emi sat in the chair and permitted me to push her around the neighborhood. It was a gorgeous spring day so many of our neighbors were outside doing yard work or playing with their children, but they were delighted to see Emi and our new acquisition. Eventually, it was Emi who demonstrated to our neighbors the wonderful features of her new mode of transportation. Later that afternoon, we took the wheelchair to the Monon Trail, and I pushed Emi along as she greeted and smiled at all the joggers and bicyclists along the trail. Every time we encountered people pushing a baby stroller, Emi would smile, call out to them, and say, "See, you never get too old to be pushed!" I was so proud of her positive attitude!

Later that week after thoroughly reading the Elderhostel newsletter she had just received, Emi booked us into a summer Elderhostel offered at the University of Oklahoma in Norman. The week-long seminar offered classes in Native American culture, regalia, and dance, culminating in attendance at the Red Earth Festival in Oklahoma City. Our collapsible wheelchair performed like it was made to travel! Pushing Emi to and from boarding gates at airports was a snap, and the friendly attendants stowed the chair in the hold and had it ready when we deplaned. It was also easy to collapse the chair and to place it in the trunk of our rental car. At the university, Emi missed nothing as I pushed her from our dorm room to various classrooms around campus. At the Cox Convention Center in downtown Oklahoma City, all activities at Red Earth, our nation's largest pow-wow, were accessible, and Emi and I thrilled to the expert dancing, colorful regalia, spirited drummers, and lively singers. In the vendors' hall, we marveled at the displays of Native American art, sculpture, and crafts. Following our trip to Oklahoma, the wheelchair was always in the car or airplane, no matter where we traveled!

As Emi realized how valuable the walker and wheelchair were to her quality of life, her lifestyle, and her safety outside, I hoped that she would see the wisdom of using a cane or walker indoors as well, but that didn't happen. "I can just hang on to things inside," she insisted anytime I brought up the subject. "Everything is so close in the house." The trouble was that as I observed Emi move through the house, she didn't hang on to furniture or door jams! She owned three canes and an indoor walker, but for the most part, they lay in corners gathering dust.

The end result was that Emi fell frequently no matter how much I tried to protect her. She was stubborn and determined not to become weak and helpless. So she continued to fall, often and hard. No matter where I was in the house, as soon as I heard Emi exclaim, "Oh, damn," I knew she was down. Sometimes, we tried to find humor in the situation, as when she fell fully-clothed into her bathtub, or when she fell outside behind the perennial garden where she could not be seen and yelled to passers-by, "Help! I've fallen and I can't get up!" But as Emi aged, falling became no laughing matter.

I learned early on that nothing is more frustrating than trying to protect someone you love so completely from physical harm. Unfortunately, Emi became known for her falls. We had the fire department just two blocks away on speed dial. The firefighters knew the way to our house, no directions needed! Our next door neighbors were also willing to come running to pick her up. It was a good thing because most of her falls occurred while I was at work.

Shortly after her eightieth birthday, Emi, using no walker or cane, stepped outside on the front porch with her three-month-old birthday puppy Frosty on a leash. Suddenly, the puppy bolted toward a young child who was walking by, and pulled Emi clean off the porch so quickly that she had no time to protect her face, which smashed into a metal garden hose coupling. By the time I arrived home from school, our next-door neighbor Tina and her nurse sister-in-law were bandaging Emi's face! For weeks afterwards, she resembled a raccoon!

Another time, Emi lost her balance and fell backwards off the porch onto large, limestone pavers that lined the garden. I was unlocking the front door and turned back toward her just in time to see her fall.

Elizabeth Kidwell

She smacked her back hard on one stone, and then her head snapped forward and back, cracking on another. She began bleeding from the back of her head! Frantic, I called 911, and the operator told me not to move her and to wait for the paramedics. I placed a pillow under her bleeding head and covered her with a blanket to keep her warm while we waited for help. Two women medics arrived, examined her, picked her up, and walked her into the house. Because she took blood thinners, the paramedics worked for one half hour applying direct pressure to stop the bleeding.

Emi fell everywhere. She fell in her bedroom in the middle of the night, cracking her head on her marble-top dresser. She tripped on the edge of a rug in the living room, fell to the floor, snapping a rib in two. She dropped in the driveway, at parking lots, in the garden, in the hallway, in the kitchen, in every room of the house, in fact.

The most devastating fall occurred in 2003. While I was at school, Emi rose from her desk in the living room too quickly, passed out, fell backwards, and smacked the back of her head on the edge of a hardwood end table before crumpling to the floor. When she regained consciousness, she walked into her bedroom to take her afternoon nap. There is a reason, I learned later, that doctors do not advise people to sleep following a brain injury or concussion. By the time I arrived home in the late afternoon, Emi was still sleeping, yet usually she was awake this time of day, eager to welcome me home. Thinking that she was extra tired or just took her nap later than usual, perhaps delaying it to finish a good book, it was dinner time before I finally woke her up. She then told me about her fall and showed me the huge goose egg on the back of her head, tender to the touch. I put an ice pack on the injury, but the damage had already been done.

As weeks turned into months, I began to notice subtle changes in Emi's usually happy and upbeat personality, so imperceptible that I was not alarmed at first. However, as more months passed, the changes became too serious to ignore, but by that time, it was too late for medical intervention. Emi became belligerent toward and suspicious of long-time friends. She accused them of stealing belongings important to her, and while our friends and I would show her that her treasures still lay where she always kept them, within a half-hour, she would forget and start accusing them and complaining to me again. The saddest time of all that year occurred when Emi even began to mistrust me. It was a very difficult time for us both.

Then suddenly, after about a year, she snapped out of it, and I got my Emi back! Something that had turned off in her brain from the fall was suddenly switched back on! I was never more grateful.

Two weeks after Emi died, the mortuary called to say that Emi's cremains were ready for pick up. Louise had just flown home to California, so I called my friend Ann. She had told me that four days before she died, Emi had made Ann and her husband Richard promise to look out for me. My sister Louise had also asked for the same promise from her, so Ann and Richard became my guardian angels. "You stay right there," Ann ordered, now always very protective of me. "I will be right over to take you. You have no business driving there by yourself." When we arrived at the mortuary, I quickly paid the balance for the cremation and in return received a small, plain, white cardboard box weighing about five pounds. On top of the box was a white sticker bearing Emi's name. I held the box lovingly on my lap all the way home, and though usually chatty, Ann was respectfully quiet. She pulled into my driveway, walked me to the door, and accompanied me into the house, staying just a few minutes to make sure that I was all right. I wasn't all right at all, but I faked it.

When Ann was gone, I carried the box upstairs and placed it in the middle of my empty desk. There it sat for a week, a daily reminder to me of my great loss. Finally, I mustered up enough courage to take a look. Slowly and sadly, I lifted the lid and stared down at what remained of my Emi through the clear plastic bag inside. What I saw horrified me beyond words, and I burst into tears, wailing out loud in my grief.

Here, I thought to myself, I had spent twenty-five years trying to protect Emi from broken bones. I was very proud of the fact that she had never broken an arm, a leg, or a hip on my watch. Yet what the crematory had done to her was to crush every bone in her body! I couldn't bear to look at this pile of crushed bones and teeth. Recovering my composure, I took out a small silvery bucket with a matching lid and handle. It had once contained gourmet popcorn which Emi

Elizabeth Kidwell

had eaten and enjoyed! How appropriate, I thought, and I knew that Emi would have enjoyed the irony of what I would do next. I lifted the sealed plastic bag out of the box. Then, I transferred Emi to the silvery bucket and closed it securely with the lid. Since she had "kicked the bucket" I thought sadly, I'll put her in one! I knew she would appreciate the humor. For the next three years I kept her close to me, on the lower shelf of the bedside table, until I mustered the courage to take her to her final resting place in Turkey Run State Park.

Wounded Wings

As you aged, frequently you fell
And every tumble took its toll,
Bruising my heart
As you bruised your body.

Because you could not rise alone,
I would always pick you up,
Hold you close, and cry inside
As little pieces of you slipped away.

Whenever I inspected the damage,
Swollen face, broken bones,
Black and blue testimonials to pain,
A piece of me would slip away as well.

Older and older, you continued to drop painfully,
Leaving a blood trail for me to follow.
I could bind up your wounds, gauze and tape,
But my own hurts bled freely and never closed.

If only I could have given you soft landings,
Or crashed to the earth for you instead,
My precious falling star,
Gladly would I have fallen for you.

Now gone from me, you collapse no more,
But still I find a crater in my heart
Where you plunged with reckless love
Into the life of a woman now fallen.

Chapter 11
Hair

From the age of five, my red hair was always cut short. Long, it tended to snarl, and I always set up a howl after my mother shampooed it and my dad dried it energetically with a towel, and then combed out the tangles that he had created. With the onset of school, it was just easier on my parents and me to keep it short. As I grew, my hair became heavy like wire so that, thankfully, it lay wherever it was combed. Besides that, I spent most of my summers swimming in lakes, rivers, oceans, and pools, so it just made sense to keep it short. By the time I began my teaching career, my hair style was set: straight wiry hair with sweeping bangs and sides long enough to cover my ears.

When I met Emi, her hairstyle had also been set in her childhood. She wore her hair short, but unlike mine, her hair was naturally curly. Short brown ringlets shot with a little gray lay beautifully all over her head, framing her sweet, round face and covering her ears, which jutted out, she often said, like a rhesus monkey's! One of my favorite past times was to run my fingers lovingly through her soft curls. She liked it too!

As I entered menopause, my hair texture gradually changed. It became lighter and softer again, so that the wind began to play with it. It only took a slight breeze to toss my hair aloft and out. My hair was clearly out of control, and I was allergic to hairspray. Allowing it to grow seemed the best option, but suddenly more serious matters intruded on my decision.

Emi and I had been in love for six years when we faced our first health crisis. Early in the summer of 1994, I was diagnosed with uterine cancer! The large tumor that filled my uterus was a combination of carcinoma and sarcoma, two deadly forms of cancer, a biopsy revealed. Surgery for a radical hysterectomy was scheduled for six weeks later, but I wanted the operation right away. "If I operate now," my surgeon explained, "the tumor will metastasize and spread throughout your body. The biopsy incision must have time to heal before surgery is performed." He also told me that the tumor could have eaten its way through the back wall into the bowel, and that I might wake up after the surgery with a colostomy bag. "I will also have to take a few lymph nodes from both sides of your groin," he added sadly. I was both stunned and alarmed by the news. If Emi was shaken by the news, she didn't show it. Always my rock, she hugged me close and suggested that we go on our annual summer vacation.

With six weeks of time on our hands, we decided to go forward with vacation plans. I told Emi that I needed to travel to the sacred Black Hills of South Dakota. There, I explained, I wanted to perform a private four directions Lakota pipe ceremony to ask the Creator for the strength to face this difficult journey on which I found myself. I discovered that the ritual and words for this ceremony were clearly explained in the Lakota holy man's book, *Black Elk Speaks*, which I had been reading. By this time in our relationship, our Native American practices and beliefs were integrated into our personal spiritualties. Together, Emi and I planned our spirit journey. Emi researched the area and the roads that we would travel.

Our first planned stop would be the Pipestone National Monument in Minnesota. Pipestone contained protected quarries where the Lakota and other Native American tribes have traditionally mined a soft red stone called catlinite. The Lakota artisans use the red stone to carve the small bowls for their ceremonial peace pipes. A week later when Emi and I arrived at Pipestone, we descended into the quarry. There, a single Lakota man with long, flowing, black hair worked alone, searching for just the right stone for his pipe making. We greeted him warmly, and he kindly showed us his tools and the different hues in the catlinite that he was mining. I shared with him my Cherokee ancestry, adding that we were on our way to the sacred Black Hills so that I could celebrate a private pipe ceremony to ask for healing and courage. The Lakota man looked into my eyes kindly and spoke respectfully, "You are going to the right place. My people call the Black Hills the *paha sapa,* which means 'the heart of everything that is.' You will surely find the Great Spirit there."

"I have the ceremony I will be using," I explained, "but I have no pipe or tobacco."

Helpfully, he added, "You will find what you need at the visitor's center near the entrance to this monument."

Emi and I thanked him and climbed uphill to the center. There we found dozens of beautiful Lakota pipes carved by local artists. After admiring their expert workmanship for quite some time, I chose a simple four directions pipe with four carved infinity rings encircling the top of the bowl. I also purchased a pouch of sacred tobacco and a pouch of shredded red willow bark. Satisfied that I had what I needed, Emi and I continued on our westward journey.

Seventy-eight miles into South Dakota on Interstate 90, Emi and I noticed a strange building towering over the rolling plains. Signs along the way advertised the Corn Palace in Mitchell. As we drove closer, the building's Russian onion domes and minarets beckoned to us. Always ready for a new adventure, we could not resist the call of this unusual building. We explorers discovered that this unique edifice was constructed of concrete. The interior auditorium was used for sporting events, rodeos, and concerts, while the exterior of this palace was covered in corn! The delightful outdoor corn murals centered around a theme each year. These interesting works of art were designed using twelve different natural colors of corn grown by a local farmer. Best of all, we learned that the corn murals served as the world's largest bird feeder! As winter sets in and snow covers the plains, hundreds of birds and squirrels feed off the corn on the murals, so that the corn murals must be replaced each year by artists, who create their masterpieces following a theme. Happily, this strange, unscheduled, surprise attraction lifted our spirits and put smiles on our faces!

Our next stop was a scheduled visit to Badlands National Park, a fossil-rich park where over eighty-four distinct species of Oligocene animals, including camels, had been recovered by paleontologists. The day Emi and I visited, we were lucky enough to observe an active "pig dig," as scientists and archaeologists worked carefully to uncover a large prehistoric pig fossil skeleton. The diggers were kind as they explained to us the steps they were taking to preserve this unusual animal fossil. Once again our visit to this mysterious park distracted us from our concerns over my impending surgery. Determined to learn what this journey had to teach us, we traveled on.

Emi and I had reserved a motel room in Custer, South Dakota, and it became our home and headquarters during our two-week stay. From that location, we ventured out on day trips to explore the sacred site of Bear Lodge, also called the Devil's Tower in Wyoming, and in South Dakota, we visited Rapid Creek, the Black Hills, Spearfish Canyon, Mount Rushmore, Crazy Horse Monument, the town of Deadwood, Wind Cave, and especially Custer State Park. In this park, we were thrilled by the sight of so much wildlife: bison, elk, pronghorn antelope, bighorn sheep, deer, wild burros, and prairie dogs. We explored several scenic roads through the park and marveled at its colorful, breathtaking views. Yet always in the back of my mind lay the urgency to perform my four-direction Lakota pipe ceremony. Little did I realize that this ceremony would be the most spiritual experience of my life.

One afternoon, as Emi prepared to take a much-needed nap, I told her that I was going to drive to Custer State Park for my pipe ceremony. She smiled warmly, hugged me close, kissed me, and spoke softly, "I love you, Darling. Go, and everything will be all right." I squeezed her in response, feeling safe in the security of her total love.

As I drove into the park ten minutes later, I had no idea where I was going to perform the ceremony or where I would find secluded privacy. I continued on for a mile or two until I noticed to my right a huge stone outcrop surrounded by trees. Immediately, I felt drawn to this place, thinking that it might provide the privacy that I required. I parked the car at the base of the outcrop, and gathered my pipe, tobacco, bark, matches, and book, placing them carefully inside a green, cloth book bag. Then I climbed upwards toward the massive rocks. I was surprised to emerge from the brush and trees into a secluded clearing, completely concealed by a massive gray boulder on one side and by a stand of tall green pines on the other. Upon closer inspection, I was delighted to discover a convenient natural table ledge at the base of the bare rock. There, I reverently placed my sacred objects and then turned, allowing my eyes to sweep the entire area. It is perfect, I thought. This is where I am meant to be!

I began my spirit journey reverently by offering a gift of sacred tobacco to each of the four directions, beginning with the East and turning clockwise, ending with offerings of tobacco to both Mother Earth and Father Sky. I continued by facing the East again, offering special prayers to the guardian spirits and to the Great Mystery. As I turned toward the East, a medium-sized, rust-colored mammal with yellowish fur on its belly appeared out of the rocks. It stared at me apparently unafraid and lingered during the entire prayer as if it was joining me in praise to the Creator. Unfamiliar with the animal, I later identified it as a yellow-bellied marmot. As I turned toward the South, a northern cardinal flew from the trees and landed on a large rock directly in front of me. The red bird also sat reverently and attentively, as if listening to my prayer. Only when I finished my invocation did he fly off.

When I faced the West, the direction representing darkness and the end of life, my body, inexplicably, uncontrollably, began to shake all over. The wind picked up and a cloud blew over, blocking the sun and darkening the sky. Despite my alarm, I bravely continued to face the darkness of the West, and trembling, voiced my prayer, fully aware that I was confronting my own inner darkness and the end of life. As I finished, the cloud moved on; the sunlight returned. Suddenly, I heard a hawk cry overhead. I looked up, and flying directly above me was my totem animal guide, the red-tailed hawk, remarkably in its red phase, a sight which I had never seen before. As I gazed directly overhead, the redhawk circled four times above me and then flew off due west! I felt comforted by the hawk's courage and stopped shaking. I realized then that I could face my cancer surgery without fear. Finally, I turned toward the North, and a little red squirrel scampered onto a tree stump in front of me! I stood quietly at first, and then voiced my prayer to the guardian spirits of the North. As soon as I finished, the tiny squirrel chattered for a minute, as if praying too, and then dashed back to the safety of the forest. After additional prayers to Mother Earth and Father Sky, I reverently lit the red willow bark in my pipe and faced each direction again, blowing the ceremonial smoke into the air representing my ascending prayers, concluding again with smoke directed toward Mother Earth and Father Sky. I realized from my spiritual experience that the Lakota people were absolutely right about the sacredness of the Black Hills! Nothing in my life prepared me for these spirit guides and the sacredness of this prayer journey.

I felt totally calm and at peace. Gathering my belongings, I walked to the car, eager now to return to the motel and to share my experience with my beloved Emi.

When I opened the door to our motel room, Emi was just awakening from her nap. I climbed into her bed, snuggled against her warm body, sharing my experiences, leaving nothing out. Emi listened with joy, her soft brown eyes and her sweet smile telling me that she was pleased, amazed, and happy for us both.

A few days later, we drove back to Indiana, fortified by our three-week vacation experiences. It wasn't long before I began to feel unseen forces at work on my behalf, securing my safety and care prior to my upcoming surgery. First, during a dental appointment, I told my dentist of my upcoming surgery. She asked me if the surgeon would be taking out my appendix, a procedure that used to be standard when women underwent this type of operation. She suggested that I ask my doctor. I called my surgeon when I returned home, and asked him. "I can take it out, no problem," he said. "I will already be in that general area, so all I have to do is tie it off, snip, and it's gone." I was heartened to hear that it would be that easy.

Next, a top gynecologist, whose children I had taught, and whom I called for a second opinion, volunteered to assist my surgeon, a personal friend of his, and to scrub in on my operation. A week later, a top surgical nurse, the mother of two other former students, traded places with another nurse so she would also be present for my surgery, along with my surgeon's red-headed nurse! I was both amazed and encouraged by the love and care of these four special people! On the day of my hysterectomy, I knew that whatever the outcome, it would be as the Creator ordained. It was a long and difficult surgery, almost six hours, I was told by my two surgeons and my two surgical nurses, my four directions guardians! Afterwards, the news was positive: the tumor seemed contained in my uterus; therefore, no lymph nodes were taken from my groin. My appendix was successfully removed, and the lab discovered that I had been suffering from acute appendicitis, which explained the periodic abdominal pain I had experienced all summer, but kept to myself. Best of all, no radiation or chemotherapy for the cancer would be required! Emi and I were elated! Happily for Emi, I had to miss the first five weeks of school, and she had me home with her for my six weeks of recovery! The only difficulty I experienced was remembering to hold a pillow to my abdomen every time I laughed, and Emi and I laughed a lot that fall!

Inspired by my spirit journey in the Black Hills and my recovery from cancer, I allowed my hair to grow long and red. Only when it reached the middle of my back, did I have the ends trimmed twice a year. Every morning after I showered and shampooed my hair, I sat on a kitchen chair, my back to Emi. Lovingly, she stood behind me and plaited my hair into one long braid down my back.

After I returned to my classroom that year, Emi kept herself busy loom-beading beautiful Native American barrettes for my long, red hair. I proudly wore her gifts every day! I once told Emi that if she died before I did, I would cut off my hair in mourning, following the Native American custom, and bury my braid with her cremains. When she left me for the Spirit World, I was true to my word. My hair has been short ever since. My long love hair was a sacred pact between us and will never be used for another.

Red

Sunrise, sunset, crimson glow.
    Garnets, rubies hold sparks
Red as the woodpecker's head.
    Cardinals, tanagers
Reflect red and scarlet rays,
    Bright as their spring voices.
Overhead maple and redbuds
    Give color to the woods,
Soon lobelia, trumpet flower,
    Strawberry, rose, and apple.
All shades and tints give forth red

    Through many seasons.
So red tresses hold my heart
    And set my blood pulsing.
        Emi

Elizabeth Kidwell

Hair

Red cascade caressing your body,
Loving you gently as I do,
First creating a sheltering drape,
Haloed heads and faces, private.
Passionate kisses meant only for us
To see and feel, eyes wide open,
Crimson hair creating a veil
Like curtains hiding a sanctuary,
The holy of holies, most sacred.
Then, as I move down your skin,
Copper tresses follow my lips, gently
Touching you in a thousand different
Places at once, rusty-colored trail
Contouring your fragrant skin,
Twin mountains and dark valley,
Legs and feet receiving equal love.

When I finish this mindful worship,
Your hands reach out parting the fall
And discover inside a glowing ark
Of pure and priceless benediction.
                  Ellie

Chapter 12
Scars

Until my cancer surgery, I carried only one little scar on my body, a tiny indent at the tip of my right index finger. It was left there by our family physician, Dr. Tetley, who lanced it when I was in sixth grade. I had developed an infection under my fingernail, an interesting color combination of yellow and green pus that caused my finger to swell painfully. It was my first trip to the doctor that I could remember, and I had no fears or expectations. So when the kindly doctor used his scalpel to lance my sore finger, I experienced my first lesson in skin trauma. Searing pain throbbed as pus exploded from the wound and continued to increase as he peeled the damaged skin from around the tip of my finger. I immediately felt faint as the light around me began to grow dim, and Dr. Tetley quickly laid me back on the examination table so I wouldn't black out. Satisfied that he had removed all infected tissue and drained all the infection, he bathed my finger in disinfectant and bandaged it in white gauze and adhesive tape to twice its normal size.

When we arrived home, my mother fixed my sack lunch and drove me to school. I spent the rest of the day amazed at all the attention I received from my teachers and classmates, as they admired my huge white bandage. Proudly, over and over, I described my encounter with the doctor's scalpel and how brave I had been. I healed quickly after that, and in a few weeks' time, my pain subsided and only the tiny scar reminded me of what I had suffered.

Many years later, when Emi and I crowned our six-month friendship with passionate intimacy, I was oblivious to the scars that crisscrossed her body until almost six weeks later when our heat for each other cooled slightly to sweet caressing and exploration. What I discovered clearly on her body at first alarmed me. A huge, ragged, twelve-inch scar ran from Emi's pubic bone to her navel! It gleamed white, at least one-half inch wide. I had nothing to compare it to. "How did you get that scar?" I inquired, very concerned.

"Oh, I had cancer in my small intestines and had to have a section of it removed, and I also had a hysterectomy," she explained in a far away voice.

Gazing lovingly at her body, I began to notice other ragged scars as well: a semi-circular one curved around the nipple of her right breast. "And this one?" I continued, pointing at her scarred breast, totally interested now.

Emi answered immediately in words that sounded somewhat rehearsed. "Oh that? I had a benign tumor in my breast that had to be removed many years ago." She tried to sound nonchalant, but I wasn't fooled. Even decades ago, I knew, surgeons prided themselves in straight incisions causing minimal scarring. There were other shorter scars on her chest, abdomen, and arms, and tiny, star-shaped scars dotted her arms and back. Whoever did this to her was a butcher, I sadly concluded and decided not to ask further.

Weeks later, when Emi was finally permitted to tell me the truth, she admitted that her former explanations were bogus. The truth was that some of her spy missions were terribly dangerous and painful. In 1961, during a mission in Vietnam, she explained, a ruthless man, whose sex trafficking operation she was infiltrating, took a large knife and ripped her abdomen from her pubic hair to her belly, doing serious damage. Helpless, she had to be rescued by twelve Marines, six of whom lost their lives while saving her. "Yes, there was extensive damage," she finally admitted, "and I almost died." Her intestines had to be re-sectioned and a radical hysterectomy performed, but not because of cancer. After a long recovery under the care of her loving parents, she was secretly summoned to Washington, D.C., where she received her first Purple Heart from President John F. Kennedy in a private ceremony.

The breast scar, she explained, was the result of another mission in Southeast Asia. A malevolent man, whose murderous business she had also infiltrated, grew suspicious, grabbed a knife, and began to cut off her right nipple. Immediately, Emi told me, her training kicked in. She reached up, grabbed his head, twisted it, and snapped his neck. When the evil man's woman accomplice rushed at her with a knife, Emi had to disarm and kill her as well.

The additional scars all had similar origins, but the star-shaped scars were the result of a flogging she had received during another mission. The whip used was tipped with small pieces of sharp metal, which ripped tiny holes in her skin all over her body. Emi even had a disfigured thumb nail on her left hand, the result of being shot when she raised her hand to defend herself. It was then that I realized how insignificant my own little scar and ailments were. Sadly, I listened to every story, proudly realizing what a precious, courageous hero I held in my arms.

The most serious scars Emi carried, I gradually learned, were the invisible ones on her heart, mind, and soul. She was deeply scarred by the horrors of the evil acts and the ugliness of the enemies she bravely faced during the long decades of her national service.

In the evenings, Emi always retired earlier than I did. Often, her peaceful sleep was blasted by horrifying dreams, and she would call out, her voice speaking a language I did not know. She had warned me repeatedly not to wake her in the middle of a nightmare, so I would stand at her bedroom door and listen, carefully approaching her only when she quieted and I felt her emerge from sleep. Only then would I sit on the side of her bed, gather her in my arms, and hold her until gradually she slipped back into a peaceful sleep, breathing softly once again. Emi enjoyed owning weapons of every kind, but because of her PTSD, none were ever stored in her bedroom.

I could not even begin to imagine the physical pain that Emi had suffered, but I did understand how scarred she was inside. At least once a week, she visited an Army psychiatrist for counseling sessions at Fort Benjamin Harrison while I was at work. When she went, she wore Army fatigues bearing a last name not her own, reminding me that she was "a ghost" in intelligence terminology. That uniform hung in the back of her closet for years until she retired from active service and switched to a civilian therapist.

I believe that for Emi the most difficult part of working for the Army Intelligence Service was the lack of public recognition. She had received medals and awards in closed ceremonies at the White House over the decades she served. She had been personally decorated by

Presidents Truman, Eisenhower, Kennedy, Johnson, Ford, Carter, Reagan, and Bush, and by Chairman of the Joint Chiefs of Staff, Colin Powell, as well as by several generals and colonels.

While Emi struggled in therapy to be proud of her service to our country, she suffered intense remorse for the unexpected, horrible acts she had to carry out as part of her duty. Once again, our Native American spirituality enabled her to gain recognition and to experience pride in the secret acts she had performed. We began to attend Indian pow-wows, a celebration of native life and honor to the Creator in the form of drumming, singing, and dancing. At our first pow-wow, Emi and I learned that the second dance, which followed the Grand Entry, was always the Veterans Dance. When the dance was announced, all military veterans, native or not, were invited to enter the Sacred Circle. Emi and I watched fascinated as dozens of men and women approached the East entry to join Native American veterans in the dance of honor. As the drumming and singing began, the head dancers led the military warriors clockwise around the circle. At the conclusion of the song, the drums and the dancers stopped. The master of ceremonies then invited all attendees outside the circle to enter, if they wished, to offer thanks to the men and women who had served in the military. Hundreds of people did so, weaving in and out among the veterans to offer their thanks both with words and a special handshake.

Emi was amazed and captivated by what she witnessed. From then on at each pow-wow we attended, two or three a year, she proudly danced the Veterans Dance and rightfully received thanks for her service. Eventually, she wore a long native skirt and carried a red shawl specially decorated with the image of a black bear, her personal totem animal. For many years Emi received the thanks and appreciation of thousands of Americans for her service to her country, although they had no idea what her service had entailed. Dancing the Veterans Dance became so important to Emi's healing, that even after walking became painful because of her neuropathy, she continued to dance using her outdoor walker. Eventually, when she could no longer walk and dance, I enabled her to participate by pushing her around the dance area in her wheelchair on the soft grass of the Sacred Circle. I would leave her side only to honor and to thank the other veterans, but she was always first.

As I joined hundreds of other people who entered the circle in thanking her and many other veterans for their service, risking their lives to save ours and to ensure our freedom, my heart and my mind swelled with pride for my Emi. I hoped each time that the recognition she received and people's kind words would help her mind and heart to heal. My love for her was huge, and often I would feel humbled when I realized that such an important woman chose me to love.

Years later when death claimed my Emi, I personally discovered a new kind of bleeding and scarring. Welling from deep within my innermost core, a searing pain tore me up. No pain medication or bandage could help me or ease the outpouring of grief. Out of control, I bled the pure emotion of loss. Tears streamed down my face, soaking my clothes and depleting my energy. Death had already claimed many family members and friends in the past. Their loss made me very sad, and I had cried, but nothing prepared me for the pain that losing the love of my life would cause. I suffered utter agony, which has no words. Grief felt like half my body and soul had ceased to exist, and I was just dragging around the useless other half like a burden.

At times I even prayed for death, so strong was my wish to join her. I realized, however, that my Emi had given me the best example. She had loved life right up until the very end. I knew she expected me to carry on, but how, I wondered, could I do that without her?

Wounded Wings

The map of your
Service patriotic
Was written on your body.
I could follow each mission
Tracing with gentle finger, the
Scars,
Grim reminders of pain,
That crisis-crossed your
Soft skin,
Many white highways
Leading nowhere.

Those silent witnesses
To violent pain
Left clear avenues,
Easy to follow, and
I often kissed my way
Quietly
Along the
Marked footpaths
To thank you
For your sacrifice.

Perhaps you lay there,
Reliving
The horror of your wounds

Elizabeth Kidwell

As I traveled these
Little roads, hoping
To give you comfort.

You never said.
But with tender touch
And so much love, I
Took these short journeys
To bring you only healing.

Chapter 13
Dancing Rainbows

From childhood I have always delighted in the sight of a rainbow. There is a mysterious happiness, a joy that arises in me at the sight of one. Perhaps it is their rarity that makes them so precious to me. In grade school I had studied rainbows, their causes, and their seven predictive colors that my classmates and I memorized easily using the memory name, Roy G. Biv for red, orange, yellow, green, blue, indigo, and violet. Single rainbows, fire rainbows, and the twice-awesome double rainbows always mesmerized me by their beauty, unpredictability, and surprise. Whenever a rainbow appeared in the sky, I thanked the Creator because what I saw in each one was not just the seven colors, but the miracle of each color blending so subtly with the next so that it was difficult to discern where one color ended and the next one began. The message I fully sensed in the presence of a rainbow was that all of life blends together in the harmony of an eternal circle.

It wasn't until I met Emi, however, that I learned how rainbows could be created using crystal prisms. I vaguely remembered a science textbook photo of a prism, but reality often teaches the lesson best. One early November morning, during a weekend visit with Emi in her large house on the Northside of Indianapolis, I noticed an unusual free-standing, antique-looking glass prism sitting on the sash of the east-facing window in her living room. I asked her about it, and she explained that it had belonged to her father Raymond, who had enjoyed his career as a high school biology teacher. When he retired, she told me, he brought it home from his classroom. "Why do you have it sitting on the window casement?" I asked.

"You'll see, Darling," she responded. A knowing smile flitted across her sweet face.

An hour later, a brilliant late fall sun rose over the neighbor's roof across the street, its rays striking the prism at just the right southeast angle. Instantly, a dozen rainbows burst from the facets, scattering across the room, delighting my vision! I have never met anyone who could refrain from smiling at the sight of so much colorful beauty. Sure enough, as I looked over at Emi, and she at me, pure joy lit up our faces. "Rainbows!" we both shouted simultaneously.

Well, the secret of my delight was out, and Emi, as usual, went overboard in trying to please me. At that time, a large chandelier hung from the ceiling of Emi's dining room. It had been transplanted there from her grandparents' Victorian entryway as her inheritance. To fit it into her low-ceiling dining room, workmen had removed a few dozen crystals. As it was, tall visitors often bumped into it anyway because Emi had no dining room table and chairs. A tall hemlock tree outside blocked sunlight from striking the chandelier, so no rainbows.

The next time I stayed at Emi's house, she handed me a small box. When I opened it, I discovered several different-shaped crystals from her chandelier. Smiling, I gave her a big hug. "Thank you," I said, "but what do I do with them?"

"We are going to hang them in the south-facing window in the living room at your house!" she explained enthusiastically, hugging me back. She gathered a hammer, a box of small finishing nails, and a spool of thick cotton thread. "You bring the prisms," she added with a smile and a wink.

When we arrived at my house, we parted the short drapes covering the front window. Emi climbed on my safety ladder, and as I handed the nails to her, she hammered them gently into the top of the wooden window frame, leaving a couple of inches of space between each one. Next, she directed me to cut different lengths of thread. We looped them through the holes at the top of each prism, knotting them off. Finally, Emi climbed the ladder again and carefully placed each loop of thread over the nails, gently lowering the prisms one by one so they would not bang against the glass pane. Then, she climbed down and stepped back, observing her handiwork with a sense of pride. A half dozen prisms hung in front of the window at varying lengths. "Now what?" I asked.

"Now we wait for the sun!" she answered, grinning happily in anticipation. Emi and I sat on my sofa and waited, savoring two cups of tea, holding hands, and sharing soft conversation. Meanwhile, the late autumn sun began to wind down, and its rays lengthened as it silently traveled its downward path. A minute later the long brilliant rays struck the window pane, shot through the prisms, and exploded from the facets into a hundred miniature rainbows that instantly decorated the walls, carpet, and ceiling of my living room. Amazed and delighted, I exclaimed loudly, "Whoa! Incredible!" Emi was thrilled by my reaction.

"Open your hands," she said softly after a few minutes had passed. As I did so, Emi manipulated my hands under one tiny rainbow. It looked as if I held it in my hands. Then, Emi bent over my hands and kissed the rainbow on my palms. "An early Christmas gift," she announced lovingly.

"Thank you for this gift," I whispered as I gathered her in my arms. "It is the best one I have ever received."

Eventually, when we purchased a dining room set for her house so that friends and family could join us for meals and games, Emi sold the chandelier including the additional pieces hanging in my window. "I will replace them, Darling," she promised, and she was true to her word. Every October for Emi's birthday, we drove to Brown County State Park, eating a gourmet picnic lunch amid the colorful foliage. Later in the afternoon, we drove into Nashville, Indiana, to investigate the contents of the tiny tourist shops and to crown our day with dinner, eating fried chicken and fried biscuits with apple butter at the Nashville House Restaurant. As we walked around the town, one shop in particular caught our attention. In its clear glass windows hung dozens of Swarovski clear, lead-free, two-inch prisms. We entered the shop, pleased to find so many prisms to choose from, each cut in varying shapes and facets. Emi left my side, and while I was admiring the prisms, she was at the counter, speaking with the clerk. A few minutes later, she rejoined me at the window. "Put out your hand," she insisted. I did so, and immediately Emi placed a crystal, heart-shaped prism into my palm. "Just so you know," she explained, "you always have my heart."

Over the next couple of years, we returned to that shop often, and each time Emi bought me a new prism. My front room window began to resemble the window in the shop! Best of all, when the sun's rays hit just right, my life was enriched again with hundreds of miniature rainbows. Not satisfied with the knowledge she had shared, Emi taught me how to make the rainbows dance by winding the prism on the thread in one direction and letting go. As the prisms unwound, the rainbows leapt to life, adding another dimension of fun and wonder to our joy!

Following my cancer operation in 1994, Emi decided that it was time for me to move in with her. While packing, I carefully wrapped each prism in soft Kleenex, storing them in a small box. Unpacking after the move, I carefully placed the box with the prisms in the bottom drawer of a dresser in Emi's upstairs library. Very soon, my life became too busy even to think about hanging them in a window again.

Years later, as part of my grief therapy following Emi's death, my therapist Ellen suggested that I try drawing a mandala. Interested, I did some research online and discovered that the word "mandala" comes from the Sanskrit word for "circle" or "completion." I realized that I was no stranger to the mandala because Native American spirituality centers around the belief in the Sacred Circle of Life, the Medicine Wheel, a deeply meaningful concept, the symbolism of the lessons found and learned in nature. Eternal life is repeated over and over, no beginning, no ending, ever changing, the one constant. The "circle with a center" is the basic pattern of Creation, the Infinite. While I understood it, I was not motivated to create my own representation. I was invited to draw an image that would allow my feelings and emotions to come through. The problem was that I was not encouraged. I was not inspired. I was empty. So, I put the idea of the mandala aside and continued my aimless wanderings around the silent house, bursting into tears whenever the sight of a meaningful object triggered a memory of my life with Emi.

One morning about two months after I lost Emi, I was investigating the contents of the drawers in the library that had become my office, now furnished with both a computer center, a separate teacher's desk, and two queen beds for guests. I was opening and closing each drawer in the room, realizing that they contained enough stuff to open a small store. As I peered into the very bottom drawer of the last bureau, a small golden box caught my eye, and immediately I realized why. I lifted the box out and raised its lid. What I expected to find were six Swarovski prisms. What I found were just three. Conspicuously absent was the first one Emi gave me: her crystal heart. Of course, I set up a fresh wailing at my loss. How could I not? As usual, I descended the two flights of stairs to the basement, where I could wail freely without alarming the neighbors. I half expected to find those prisms while cleaning out the rest of the house, but I never did. Their loss remained a mystery, but in my heart I hoped that they were bringing the joy of countless rainbows to others.

Later that day, when I had recovered, I again opened the box and took stock of the three remaining prisms: an appropriate teardrop one, an oval drop, and a clear crystal ball. The heavy, white thread was still looped through the holes at the top of each. I walked to the south-facing window and removed the half curtains supported by a tension rod, placed the prisms' loops over the rod, and hung it back in the window. The sun was just setting so I decided to check back in the morning.

I awoke a little before 8:00 the next morning and stumbled sleepily down the hall to the office/guest bedroom. As I opened the door, bright colored light exploded in front of my eyes! Everywhere was a rainbow! It had been twenty years, but the effect was the same: wonder, joy, peace. I allowed my eyes to wander across the walls and ceiling to the white cotton spreads on the two guest beds: rainbows of various shapes lay everywhere I looked! The blessing was back! I climbed onto the bed closest to the window and lay back. Instantly, I was covered in tiny rainbows. I imagined that each rainbow was a kiss from my Emi, and her love once more flooded over me. I luxuriated in that happy feeling for quite some time. Then I sat up and reached up, winding the crystal ball. I released it, and the rainbows danced once more! When you are in love, time is always the present. In the presence of the dancing rainbows, I felt the warmth of my Emi's love all around me, and I was comforted. "Yes, haunt me!" I whispered to her spirit.

A few days later, I climbed the stairs to the office room late in the afternoon. When I opened the door, color hit me in the face, but my eyes were drawn to the white ceiling. There, surrounding the space above my computer chair was a huge mandala, a perfect circle. I sat down and gazed in awe at the beautiful halo above me. Amazingly, it appeared to be made of large, rainbow colored feathers! Clearly cast through the globe prism, only the center was empty. Surely this was another gift from my Emi. Haunting me, she was!

That night I got busy. I found a perfect square of tag board in Emi's art supplies. I added a sheet of card stock, scissors, and colored pencils from my own, and I was in business. I drew a feather-shaped template on the card stock and then cut it out. Next, I used it to create twelve copies of the white feather, all exactly the same size. Using my art pencils, I colored each feather exactly the same way as I had seen them on the ceiling. I then cut out the feathers and glued each one on the tag board in a circle. Now I had my mandala, each rainbow feather representing a month of the year! At my next appointment I shared it with Ellen and explained to her the source of my inspiration. "Ordinarily," she commented, "clients draw the mandala, and the artistic act helps them to get in touch with their feelings and hopefully relax."

"Well, I am not a very good artist," I explained, "but given the Native American spirituality I shared with Emi, the creative experience was certainly meaningful to me. I just don't know yet how to complete the center."

Ellen encouraged me with her words. "Don't worry about it now. The inspiration will come, I'm sure."

When I returned home that day, I placed the tag board with the mandala upright on my desk against the bookshelf so that I could see it from all points, wherever I happened to be in the room. Weeks passed as I continued my wanderings around the house, occasionally writing poetry to express my grief, at other times shopping to buy food that I seldom ate. Such was the routine that I passed off as a life.

One afternoon I climbed the stairs to my office, now renamed the Rainbow Room, to get some envelopes. By this time I knew I could count on rainbows every sunny day. As I opened the door, I was astounded by the sight that met my eyes! There on the tag board mandala was a perfectly circular rainbow superimposed over the paper feather circle, exactly the same size!

Photo! I thought, photo! I literally flew down the stairway to grab my iPad where I had left it in the living room. By the time I sprinted up the stairs and loaded the camera app, no more than a couple of minutes had passed, but that short time had been long enough for the world to turn and for the passage of light. The circular rainbow was still cast on the mandala, but now it lay slightly off center. No matter! I took several photographs anyway. The friends I eventually showed them to were kind and amazed as I related the experience. Ellen too was equally impressed when I shared the picture with her during our next therapy session. "Once in a lifetime," she commented, studying the photo. Her words, "once in a lifetime," echoed in my mind. She had perfectly described my relationship with Emi.

Years ago you gave me
The gift of dancing rainbows.
Open your hands, you urged,
And when I did, you
Filled them with crystal
Cut glass prisms.

Then you showed me how
Prisms hanging in a south window
Split sunlight into a hundred fragments
Shooting rainbows in every direction.
We held each other for sheer delight
While brilliant color
Leapt for joy all around us, and
We marveled at the miracle.

Catching little rainbows in our hands,
We gifted dazzling color to each other,
Kissing generous palms over and over like
TREASURE.

Eventually, the sun rose higher
And the rainbows danced away.
Yet like a delighted child,
I hugged you close and thanked you for the
PRESENT.

Elizabeth Kidwell

Today, I went in search of a small box
And found the little light breakers
Quietly forgotten in a bottom drawer.
Crying at the memory, I hung them
In a light-infested window and
MAGICALLY,
They bounced to
LIFE.

And as so many years before,
Walls burst into skipping flames of
Red, orange, yellow, green,
Blue, indigo, and violet.
Not able to help myself, I was
DELIGHTED.

As before, I cupped my hands in hope,
And, as always, you dropped
A rainbow radiant love into my
HEART.

Wounded Wings

Chapter 14
Riptide

Since childhood, I had always been a strong swimmer. When I was seven, my mother, always afraid of water herself, took my younger sister Elaine and me for swimming lessons at the local pool. I loved the water and the six-week, daily summer lessons, especially since temperatures in the Great Valley of California could rise to over a hundred degrees each day. One hour in the pool each day felt like heaven to me, and I never wanted to leave. That posed a problem since I was a fair-skinned redhead. Eventually, my mother tired of my moaning and groaning every time I suffered a sunburn, and I tired of smelling like a salad from the vinegar she used on me to treat it. Since the invention of sunblock lay way in the future, the immediate solution was to wear one of my brother's white T-shirts over my swimsuit anytime I went swimming.

My sister Elaine proved to be as deathly afraid of water as my mother, so since the lessons were paid for, I got to enjoy an additional six weeks at the pool! At that time in my life, I would rather be in water than anywhere else. I especially liked holding my breath underwater. The whole world disappeared, and it was peaceful and quiet! As I grew up, anywhere my family vacationed found me seeking out the local swimming opportunities: Russian River, the American River, Rio Vista, the San Joaquin River, Stinson's Beach, and Lake Tahoe. It didn't matter to me. I enjoyed them all, although I discovered the loneliness of swimming in ice-cold Lake Tahoe, which was fed by pure snow melt, while my family stood bundled in jackets and sweaters on the pebbly beach, shaking their heads at me.

In the 1960's, California school curriculum required all high school students to participate in swimming, water sports, and life-saving as part of their daily hour of physical education classes. Antioch High School boasted a large, Olympic-sized swimming pool and an adjacent fifteen-foot diving pool. So in my sophomore year, I delighted in every water sport the school had to offer. Water polo and water volleyball were two of my favorites. It didn't bother me that our rotation to water sports occurred in November. To me, the heated pools were comfortable, although the cold, winter air quickly froze us students when we left the water, and made us appreciate the mandatory hot shower in the locker room. Following a six-week course, I passed all my exams in life-saving and water safety. The final test consisted of jumping off the fifteen-foot high dive into the deep diving pool and staying afloat by treading water for twenty minutes. This last test, I knew, safeguarded us students against the possibility that a boat or cruise ship we might be sailing on in the future would founder. The ability to jump overboard and stay afloat for at least twenty minutes until the Coast Guard or other rescuers could arrive, just might save our lives. So after passing my sophomore swimming tests, I felt like a pretty confident swimmer, and it was a good thing.

At the end of that year, my father was transferred in his job as foreman and production supervisor for Glass Containers division of the Hunt's Company to Los Angeles, and we moved. It wasn't long before I discovered the real treasures of Los Angeles County: its beaches, warm, sandy beaches! One by one, my new high school friends and I explored most of them: Malibu, Santa Monica, Marina del Rey, Playa del Rey, Manhattan Beach, Venice Beach, Redondo Beach, Hermosa Beach, and Newport Beach. I enjoyed them all, swimming to my heart's content, blessedly protected with newly-marketed sunscreen! It never occurred to me to wear a life vest. Besides, I didn't even own one!

My favorite beach was Redondo Beach with its pier containing trendy stores and my favorite seafood restaurant, Old Tony's on the Pier. At Tony's I always ordered the fried calamari, buttery, tender, and succulent. After I moved to Indiana, I heard that Old Tony's caught fire, burned down, and had to be rebuilt. Still, my favorite memory was swimming under the pier, watching the waves strike its barnacle-covered pylons.

It was while swimming at Hermosa Beach, however, that I experienced my first warning that the ocean can be unpredictable. On a weekday break from school, my friends and I decided to enjoy ourselves at this lovely beach with its warm, taupe-colored sand and its cool, refreshing waves. While my friends relaxed on shore, soaking up the sun, I swam out about a quarter-mile from the shoreline, where

I could be alone and think. Relaxed, I lay back, closed my eyes, and floated, trusting the undulating Pacific to rock me gently. The silence, I remember, was comforting.

Suddenly, I was rocked again, this time by the shrill sound of a horn, the lifeguards' warning! My eyes shot open and I righted myself as I looked toward the beach. "Shark!" I heard the lifeguards shout through their bullhorns. "Shark! All swimmers out of the water! Head in immediately! Shark! Everyone out of the water now!" Well, the blockbuster movie, Jaws would not be released until after Peter Benchley published his novel in 1974, or I may have been more alarmed. Shark attacks on the California coast in the 1960's were rare. Foolishly, I decided to give one more backward glance before heading in. I turned and saw a dark form in the water hundreds of yards away. The shape resembled the head of a California sea lion more than a shark's dorsal fin, but knowing that the presence of a sea lion could draw in large sharks, I turned and swam quickly and steadily to shore, passing the lifeguard motor boat as two of them headed out to assess the danger. When I reached the shore, my friends were already gathered to see that I got in safely. "Did you see anything out there?" they wanted to know.

"Just a sea lion," I assured them.

Fifteen minutes later the lifeguard boat returned, and the lifeguards lifted the swimming ban. "It was just a sea lion," they announced into their bullhorns, as beach goers returned to the water.

Years later in Indiana, Emi and I shared our love of swimming. She had spent her youthful summers with her parents in the 1930's at Turkey Run State Park in Indiana, where they worked as naturalists. Emi's favorite body of water was Sugar Creek, which runs through the park. Like me, Emi also spent most of her summers wet! When I first met Emi she belonged to the JCC, the Jewish Community Center in Indianapolis, and it didn't take long for me to sign up. Bedsides an outdoor heated Olympic pool, the center also maintained a beautiful indoor pool for lap swimming, water aerobics, and winter family swimming, as well as a hot tub, sauna, and showers. At least once a week, even in the winter, Emi and I enjoyed swimming side by side in the lap pool. Then we took a sauna, soaked in the hot tub, and enjoyed a luxurious, hot shower. By the time we returned home, we were clean, exercised, and relaxed. This remains as one of my favorite memories of our life together.

For me, living in the eastern half of the United States afforded me the opportunity to explore more bodies of water: the Great Lakes, the Atlantic Ocean, the Caribbean Sea, the Mississippi River, Lake Champlain, the St. Lawrence Seaway, and the Everglades! During my spring breaks from school, Emi and I spent many of them in Florida. For our very first vacation in the Sunshine State together, we flew to Fort Myers, rented a car, and drove to Sanibel Island, where we had reserved a two-bedroom condominium near Bowman's Beach. The condo was fully appointed, so we prepared most of our meals there.

Our week on the island was magical. Bowman's Beach was a shell collector's paradise. The inter-coastal canal between our condo and the beach was home to a great variety of wildlife, including alligators, wood storks, anhingas, white pelicans, and roseate spoonbills. In addition, Emi and I spent several early mornings at J.N. "Ding" Darling Wildlife Refuge, which comprised almost half the island. The refuge is home to over 245 species of birds, and using our binoculars and spotting scope, we saw our fair share! About every fourth bird was a lifer for me including mangrove cuckoos, black scoters, limpkins, Bonaparte's gulls, black skimmers, royal terns, fish crows, snowy egrets, tricolored herons, white ibis, common gallinules, purple gallinules, common moorhens, and a remarkable albino great blue heron! It was a bird watcher's paradise, and although Emi had been here before, she thoroughly enjoyed showing me the beauty and wonder of it all!

Every morning during that magical week, I awoke early and walked to Bowman's Beach, carrying a sack for shell collecting. I had the beach all to myself, watching as the white, foamy surf scoured the sand. The beauty and the variety of the shells were amazing, the colors brilliant and varied, and I was greedy for their loveliness. When I returned to the condo to share my finds with Emi, she too marveled at them with me, doubling my wonder! I had never loved Emi more! Our love of life and nature bound us even closer, a union that would never be broken. In the midst of so much love, joy, and beauty, death was the last thing we were thinking of. If humans were allowed to choose their time of death, looking back now, the day after this vacation week on Sanibel would have surely been my choice. As it turned out, I almost got my wish.

It was our last day on Sanibel, and since we had worn ourselves out exploring and enjoying all the island had to offer, we decided to spend the day at Bowman's Beach, swimming, reading, picnicking, and soaking up a little sun. By early afternoon we had eaten lunch, and Emi was content to curl up on her beach towel with a good book. This early April day had turned warm, and naturally, I was eager to swim. As I happily walked down the rise and entered the water, dying was the last thing on my mind. I waded out into four feet of salt water, smiling at the young children playing beach ball catch with their father about ten feet away. But I never had a chance to dive into the surf.

Suddenly without warning, a malevolent force snapped my legs out from under me, slamming my body to the sand and sucking me out to sea! At the same moment, a high wave crashed over me, engulfing me and cutting off my air supply. As I struggled to stand, the force grabbed at me again. A second, stronger wave crashed over me, slamming my face into the sand and leaving me no chance to breathe. Once again I felt incredibly strong water hands dragging my legs seaward. I realized then that I had never faced a force, an adversary this strong, and despite my swimming skills, I felt helpless against it. The more I struggled to take a breath, the more the ocean fought to have me. By the time a fourth wave flattened me, I knew that I was really in trouble. Growing weak and desperate in my struggle, I sought just one breath to gather my strength. Instead, I inhaled a mixture of water and sand. It was at this point that I realized that I was going to drown. Whatever had me in its grasp would suck me out to sea, and I would never be heard from again. I could not imagine why the people playing next to me were not coming to my rescue, unless they were caught in this too, and I knew that this beach had no lifeguards. I realized that Emi had her nose in her book, and unless she looked up, she would never know how hard I was fighting to return to her.

Exhausted and breathless, I began to relax and let go. The Caribbean Sea was too strong for me. Never in my life had I been afraid of water, but now I could feel real fear building up inside of me. Surprisingly, I felt peaceful as I understood that this was an appropriate end to my life. I had always loved water. Now it could have me. I closed my eyes and in my mind saw my beloved Emi sitting on the beach, sunlight playing with the soft curls on her bowed head as she sat reading. At that split second another scenario invaded my mind: Emi returning to Indiana alone, her heart broken once again, inconsolable.

If love and compassion can generate adrenalin, that is what happened to me. Instantly, a surge of pure strength I didn't know I possessed coursed through my body, giving me the courage and the energy to survive! In one mighty effort, I pulled my feet underneath me, and like a ball in a cannon, shot myself skyward into the life-giving air! Amazingly, I found myself once again standing in four feet of water, the children and their father still playing ball nearby. My legs felt weak and wobbly, as I half-walked, half-crawled up the warm sand toward the beach towel where Emi sat, still reading. I sank down beside her, and it took several minutes of sweet breathing before I could speak. "How was your swim?" Emi asked, suddenly concerned that I was taking ragged breaths.

"Deadly," I responded, after taking another deep breath so I could answer. "I almost drowned out there in just four feet of water." As I described my experience, Emi listened intently, worry lines gathering on her face.

"Darling," she said in a serious voice, "that sounds like an undertow or a rip current. How did you manage to get out of it?"

"You," I breathed softly, and then she gathered me into her arms, wet swimsuit and all!

To my overwhelming sorrow, Emi was the one who drowned, years later. Aspiration pneumonia filled her lungs with fluid, and she left me, still holding my hand. At the moment she stopped breathing, two little tears appeared, one in each eye, and I gathered them on a cotton handkerchief, knowing that they were her one last gift to me. Leaving me and the life she loved made her sad.

Elizabeth Kidwell

There you sat on Bowman's Beach,
Absorbed in a book and warmed by the sun;
While I, the more adventurous this day
Chose to swim in the wide-blue Gulf
And raced to the water's edge.

This week of spring on Sanibel
Could not have been more flawless:
Discovering life birds at Ding Darling,
Collecting shells on the shore in the early morning,
And toasting the sunset each evening.

One last day to relax before returning home,
Happily sated with love and beauty: perfect.

The salty waves lapped at my ankles
As I entered the surf and splashed my way
Toward deeper water, intent and eager
For the ministry of the ocean's cool hands
And refreshingly brisk embrace.

But a life-thief lurked in the current.
It grabbed me with forceful hands
And slammed me to the sand below.
Then it sucked the breath out of me
And brought me to my knees.

Hopelessly, I fought the death grip
That sought to pull me out to sea
As wave after wave crashed over me
And air was replaced with water and sand.
I struggled and fought, no hope of breaking free.

Wounded Wings

One last thought of you, sun-kissed on the shore...
No! My heart screamed to my head.
You cannot leave her to search alone for a lost love.
Feet gathered under me, I shot to the surface.
The salt-chains broken, life filled my lungs.

Exhausted and spent, I crawled up the warm, dry shore
And dropped my life-love beside you: perfect.

Chapter 15
Moon Woman

Emi's first partner, Beth, was an artist and an art teacher in St. Louis, Missouri. During the thirty years of their long-distance relationship, Emi was greatly influenced and enriched by Beth's artistic talent and love of art. The walls of Emi's home featured Beth's framed water colors, some dark and somber, others riotous with color. Emi had also framed two soft landscape water colors painted by Beth's grandfather and hung them prominently in the living room. During our twenty-five years together, Emi neither removed nor changed any of this precious artwork.

There were also art projects on which Emi and Beth had collaborated. One such collaboration involved casting two-inch shield-shaped crests out of lead. After Emi cast, filed, and undercoated them, she and Beth painted them. When the background colors dried, they decorated them with painted heraldic animals and beasts. The crests featured brightly-colored eagles, hawks, dragons, stags, hares, falcons, sea horses, peacocks, lions, and even a mermaid. Later, they mounted the crests against black velvet backgrounds in display cases and hung them on the walls of Emi's house after using them to illustrate their talks on heraldry for the National Button Society. So for the twenty years that Emi and I lived together in her house, I was constantly reminded of her loss. How she managed to live with these grief triggers all around her, I never knew. Clearly, she was a stronger woman than I.

When I first met Emi, she had been without her Beth for five years, and she cried whenever she spoke of her for the next five years. Sometimes, I felt as if Emi tortured herself with memories every time she looked at Beth's artwork. At other times, I noticed, the water colors seemed to comfort her. While she spoke of Beth and their shared life adventures often, I could only guess at the depth of her pain. After I moved in with Emi, she never cried again when she spoke of Beth. What I did recognize was that Emi's love for Beth burned brightly all the years I knew her and loved her, but then, so did her love for me.

At first I felt like second best, the woman Emi settled for because Beth was gone. I realized as our journey together continued that Emi would never give Beth up. Nor would I ever expect her to because I sensed early on that Emi's love for me was sparked by that eternal flame in her heart. As we grew in our loving relationship, I learned deeply along with Emi that the more people we love in our lives only enhances and magnifies the love we have for each other. Love teaches love, and longevity perfects it. So Emi and I were rich in love beyond all measure. Emi loved me well because she had over sixty years of hands-on lessons and experience by the time I met her. I had Beth to thank for much of that.

Because of her great love for Beth, our conversations often included descriptive scenes and entertaining stories from Emi's journeys with Beth in England, Africa, the Galápagos, South America, Iceland, France, Germany, Canada, Costa Rica, and many other countries. Since they were both teachers, their summer vacations had always included trips to exotic places that included birds, animals, nature, art, and beauty. Emi's stories ranged from humor to adventure, and as she aged, I listened to those same tales many times as she relived them over and over in her heart.

Since I worked full time and Emi was retired, she had much time to fill, and she never wasted the hours. In addition to her volunteer work at the Children's Museum and her many lunch dates with friends, Emi signed up for classes at the Indianapolis Museum of Art, just two miles away. In early 2003, before the fall that changed her personality and thinking for a year, Emi registered for three art classes: Paper Making, the Art of Papier-mâché, and Etching. The final project for her papier-mâché class was to create a sculpture. Emi decided that the sculpture would be her artist's hands. "I'll need your help to do it," she announced, inviting me into the creative process.

"What can I do?" I asked, immediately interested.

"I need you to apply the wet paper strips over my hands," she explained. I watched as she carefully prepared dozens of different-sized white paper strips and laid them next to a metal tray containing a wet paste mixture. "I'll direct you as we go along," she continued, sharing with me her creative vision. "The sculpture will consist of my two hands painting a lead figure of a soldier from the American Revolution." At that, she picked up a small paintbrush and a 54 millimeter Continental soldier, which she had filed, undercoated, and partially painted. Holding the little minuteman in her left hand and her brush in the right, she struck a pose with her hands. As she did so, I visualized the sculpture in my mind's eye. It would be beautiful, a real work of art. Because she was already seventy-eight, Emi's hands bore the life marks of time. Their knuckles protruded with arthritis, the swollen veins resembling small blue rivers among tiny scars that shone like stars on her brown skin. These were the hands that had loved me for sixteen years! For a moment I placed my warm hands over hers in a loving caress.

"I am proud and honored to help you immortalize these hands," I said, smiling as I leaned over to kiss her, and she met my lips with hers. Then we got to work. Emi first bathed her hands in a little cooking oil.

"So the paper doesn't stick," she explained. We sat at the kitchen table across from each other. As Emi directed me, I dipped each paper strip in the tray and gently laid strip after strip in different angles over her posed hands, lovingly and carefully smoothing them over their backs and around each finger, leaving her palms exposed underneath. I have to admit that the pottery scene from the movie *Ghost* did cross my mind. I played Patrick Swayze to Emi's Demi Moore as I caressed her hands with sticky strips. "Hey, Emi," I whispered, "remember this scene from the film *Ghost*?"

Her little moans of pleasure told me that she did. After many applications, Emi told me to stop. She sat still at the table for about thirty minutes more while we chatted happily, waiting as the glue gradually dried in the warm air and hardened the paper strips.

"I think that is enough time," she said finally. "Help me take my hands out." Slowly and carefully, she extricated her hands and fingers from the paper sculpture. Pulling the last finger carefully away, Emi and I sat back and admired her paper "Ghost Hands." Standing up to go and wash her hands, Emi hugged me and said, "Thank you for your help. I can do the rest myself. These will have to dry overnight before I can begin the next step."

By now, however, I was fascinated by her project. "What do you have to do next?" I asked.

"I just have to cover the hands with meaningful, decorative paper that reflects the theme of the art piece," she explained. "Afterwards, I will need to position and to glue the hands to a permanent wooden base that I have already chosen." From a folder lying on the table, she removed several sheets of paper. "Thom downloaded these designs and printed them off for me. I have a choice of a black and white Continental soldier design or the same design in color."

She lay the sheets of paper before me. Studying the two choices for a few moments, I had an idea and made a suggestion. "Why don't you cover your left hand holding the figure in the black and white pattern and the right one holding the brush in the colored design? Artists create in both modalities."

Emi chewed on the idea, as she studied the figures and the papers for a few minutes. "You know," she responded, "I think you might be right! Thank you for the suggestion! That's exactly what I'll do: black and white on the left hand and color on the right! Thank you, Bunting," she grinned at me, using the sweet nickname she often called me, then giving me a squeeze.

The resulting Papier-mâché sculpture was a beautiful creation. The left hand steadied the half-painted figure of a soldier, and the right hand balanced a small paint brush tipped with blue paint, just touching the figure. To me, they were the unmistakable hands of my beloved Emi, but they brought to my mind another Creator who brought nothingness to life. After Emi received her A on the project, she brought it home and placed her sculpture in a clear plastic display case on her desk, where it remained until she died.

Emi next took a class in paper-making, followed by one in etching. I helped with the paper-making class by saving clean cotton fluff in different colors from the dryer lint trap in the basement. Emi used the fluff with other secret ingredients to make different papers: dark, light, transparent, opaque, colored, white, and flecked. The paper, pressed during her classes at the art museum, was beautiful, and Emi displayed each piece in a plastic sheet protector in a large, white binder.

When Emi began her etching class, all work was completed in the classroom, so I never got to observe the process or to see Emi at her artistic best. Each week however, a new print took its place in the white binder. At first her etchings were small, printed in black ink on square scraps of colored paper provided by the instructor. Eventually, the prints grew larger, finished in colored ink on paper of different sizes and textures. Then etchings of crows, cardinals, and killer whales began to appear in the binder, beautifully matted, titled, numbered, signed, and dated.

My Emi had become an artist! From then on, Emi would entice me into her bedroom with the words, "Want to see my etchings?" Humor was another important glue that bound us close together!

For her final project, Emi created an eight-by-ten inch etching of a sad, old Indian woman sitting on a small rise. Behind her was a slash of barren tree silhouetted against the rising moon. This etching was printed in black and blue-green and entitled "Midnight Light." Emi matted one print for me, placed it in a simple frame, and gave it to me for my birthday that year. "It's my Moon Woman!" I announced excitedly, hugging Emi tightly, grateful for the gift. "She's beautiful!" From then on, the etching hung in my bedroom, and I admired it every day.

The first task that my sister Louise took on following Emi's death was to clean out and to organize her desk on the west side of the living room, a task that she knew would take me over a year of grief to complete. It only took her one day as I sat in Emi's armchair and watched helplessly as she went at it. Occasionally, Louise would bring me some legal papers to look at, but for the most part, her analytical mind had no trouble departmentalizing and organizing the desk's contents. When she finished, all important papers that required my attention were filed alphabetically in the two oak files that flanked the desk. Everything else was recycled. The other contents of the desk, mostly greeting cards and postcards, were boxed and labeled.

Louise then turned her attention to the two bookcases in the living room containing Emi's most loved books. Knowing that this task would also take me substantial grief time, she brought in several boxes which she labeled "keep" and "go." She started with the bottom shelf of the bookcase near the desk and worked her way up silently, occasionally pausing to bring me a book she thought I might want to keep. When she reached the top shelf, she walked over to me and gently, respectfully lay five thin journals into my hands. "You will want to keep these," she said, speaking softly. I took the slim volumes from her and opened each journal in turn. Emi's scratchy handwriting leaped out at me from each page.

"Yes, thanks," I whispered with difficulty to Louise, my voice catching with pain. "I need to keep these." And though I did not know the contents of these journals or why Emi wrote them, I climbed the stairs crying softly, so Louise would not know, and gave them a place of honor on the top shelf of the small bookcase above my desk. There they remained for the next year, unopened and unread.

By the time I collected myself and returned to the living room, Louise had already cleared the second bookcase and had turned her attention to the items on top of Emi's desk. Emi's personal computer was so outdated that Louise immediately erased all files and marked the PC for electronics recycling. Then, she turned her attention to Emi's Papier-mâché hands sculpture in its clear plastic case. "What about this?" she asked, not realizing what she held. As soon as she lifted it up for me to see, I burst into tears. I could not bear to look at those loving hands, absent from me now. After I recovered from my crying binge and explained to Louise about the art project, we mutually decided to put it on top of a high bookcase in Emi's separate art and library room, which I seldom entered, in order to prevent a serious case of pink eye. Thus, I did not have to look at her beloved hands daily. However, as soon as Louise returned to California the second time, I inexplicably carried Emi's masterpiece back to her desk, where I sat daily, alternately reading E. L. James's *Fifty Shades Darker* and crying. Humor especially did not help. Nothing was funny anymore. I just wanted my Emi back.

Emi's "Midnight Light" etching remained on my bedroom wall until I sold our house and moved. Following Emi's death, I truly began to feel that this sad, old Indian woman represented both of us. Until my loss of Emi, I never truly understood her loss of Beth or why it took her so long to recover. Now when I really took the time to study the artwork, I realized that not only was it a self-portrait of Emi's grief, but tragically, a mirror of my own. We were twin spirits forever in our grief. Suddenly, it came to me that Emi had never fully recovered

Elizabeth Kidwell

her loss, and I wouldn't either. A love so incredibly perfect remains alive inside a person forever. I felt a strange sense of comfort then in knowing that Emi had understood all along the anguish I would suffer when she left me. She promised to haunt me, and I guess this was part of it. Gazing at the Indian woman, I mentally felt Emi's loving embrace around my sagging shoulders.

Months later, I walked into Emi's art room and noticed a white, unmarked binder sitting on a shelf, out of place between two books. Puzzled, I picked up the binder and opened it, immediately recognizing it as the book that held all of Emi's artistic papers and etchings in her favorite plastic sheet protectors. As I leafed through her collection, I remembered them all, including the nine prints of "Midnight Light." As I turned the next page, I was suddenly caught off guard. It was obvious to me then that Emi had returned to her teacher's art classroom to create three final etchings of "Midnight Light." They were printed in simple black ink on white paper that Emi had made herself using the cotton fluff fibers from the dryer, which I had saved for her while doing our laundry. It was only as I read Emi's signature at the bottom of these prints that I noticed she had changed the name of these prints to "Moon Woman." Emi had no doubt meant to surprise me that Christmas with this new version, but before she could, her fall and subsequent cranial bleed in mid-2003, had robbed more of her short-term memory than I had realized. Yet, here was her indomitable spirit reaching across infinity once more to gift me again with love!

Sad old woman,
Bent with age and grief
And too much pain,
Slumps lost and alone beneath
A skeleton tree
As night drips slowly
All around her
Snuffing out the light.

Her dark hair flowing
Freely down her breast
Hides the sorrow in her heart.
A dark blanket hugs her close
For comfort, but the anguish
In her eyes is unmistakable,
The heartache of her sagging mouth
Fallen into woe.
While rising above her,
Round with majesty,
The moon mysterious,
A wondrous halo,
Sanctifies her sadness
And illuminates her mind,
Bearing infinite wisdom
To her in safe, reflected light.

Elizabeth Kidwell

Her future self, determined to survive
The ragged reality of loss,
Will rise surely as the moon
Romances the swelling tides.
In this holy hoop will she dance
To the beat of her own heart
Drumming in rhythm
With the song of life,
Composed of love
By sacred hands.

Wounded Wings

Chapter 16

Winter Solstice

Emi and I loved every season of the year, but winter was always an extra-special time for us. The first snowflake to hit the ground jumpstarted Emi into action. That first winter we were together, she took me shopping to ensure that my winter wardrobe matched her own. First on the list were silk long johns worn under jeans to keep the circulation going in my legs. Next, we purchased wool-blend socks, followed by strong, waterproof winter boots with excellent tread. Then Emi drove me to the Eddie Bauer outlet store where we each bought new down jackets, Emi's in purple, and mine in green, which we wore every winter for the following twenty-five years. Next on our list were wool hats, extra-thick cold weather gloves, and fuzzy ear muffs. Emi later ordered me a white, silk neck scarf to match her own. Armed with all this protection against cold weather, we spent just as many days outdoors in the winter as we did in every other season!

We loved walks in the snow holding gloved hands for love and support or walking arm in arm, the fresh-falling flakes tickling our noses. Frequently, we took a small magnifying glass with us so that we could study the unique patterns of the frozen white crystals as they landed on the purple and green backgrounds of our jackets. Often, we would make a game of catching snowflakes on our tongues like a contest. Best of all, we enjoyed our monthly picnics all through the winter, raising our mugs of hot tea or cocoa as usual to Emi's mother Marie. As always, Emi ended the toast, looking towards the sky, "Thanks, Mom!" I echoed those same words in my heart for an entirely different reason. I was totally besotted with my Emi. Sadly, I had never met Marie, but she had gifted me with her only child, my precious, priceless companion. A simple thanks would never be enough.

During the first week of December, Emi and I would visit the fresh tree lot, and at my insistence we would purchase the saddest-looking, scrawniest tree that we knew no one else would want. It bothered me to think that a young evergreen would give up its life only to be thrown into a mulch chipper on December 26. I knew that Emi preferred to buy a forty dollar beauty, but she always acquiesced to my simple reasoning. The tree lot owner often wore a puzzled look on his face when we appeared at his cash register with our pitiful choice, but in the spirit of the season, or maybe because he felt sorry for us, he never charged us more than five dollars!

When Emi and I arrived home and carried the lucky tree into the living room, she would hold it upright while I secured it at the base of the tree stand, afterwards placing it near the front window and filling the base bowl with fresh water. The wonderful smell of pine spread throughout the house. Then the transformation began! Emi would produce two plastic storage tubs from an upstairs closet, containers which held antique decorations inherited from her parents and grandparents. The ornaments were singular and charming: birds made of glass or of feathers, hand-painted glass toy soldiers in shiny red coats, shimmering glass balls covered in silver netting, and two long silver garlands. Turning the best side of the tree so that it faced the living room, we began to attach the multi-colored strings of lights, striving for an even distribution of colors before we plugged them in. Next, we carefully hung the ornaments to the tree's best advantage to compensate for bare or missing branches. We concluded our decorating by winding the silver garlands around the tree. Finally, we draped a large, red towel over the tree stand. We stepped back, arm in arm, to admire the magic transformation from pitiful to beautiful! As the December days passed, various packages, stealthily wrapped in shimmering gift paper, began to mysteriously appear at the base of the tree on that red towel, and the excitement of the season began to build in our hearts!

The day we chose to celebrate our love and this magical season was the Winter Solstice, December 21. For twenty-five years, this date was our day alone. We saw no one but each other all day and all night. It was the special time that we reveled in the incredible blessings of sharing our lives together as one: two in one!

When I awakened on the morning of Winter Solstice, I would quietly creep downstairs and climb into bed with Emi, who was usually still groggy with sleep. She would awaken gently, wrap me in her loving arms, and pull me close to her warm body. Our closeness eventually led us to making slow, gentle love, and afterwards we would lie in each other's arms, talking excitedly and happily about our special day. There was never any great hurry to this day.

Our solstice breakfast usually consisted of bacon, eggs, bakery sweet rolls, and tea. We ate hungrily as light streamed in through the kitchen picture window. Gazing outside, we enjoyed the antics of the wild birds at the feeders and of the surprised fox squirrels comically sliding down the feeder poles, which we had slicked up with cooking oil to keep them out of the birdseed! Following breakfast, we moved into the living room, switched on the solstice tree lights, and lit the logs already laid in the fireplace. We stoked the fire to blazing and kept it burning all day long. Then we took turns unwrapping our gifts to each other, oohing and awing over every present.

My gifts to Emi always included one or two breathtaking lead figures painted in oil by a talented but unknown Russian artist. I also made sure to include some jewelry or a small sculpture of Emi's totem animal, the black bear. The third gift I gave her had to include a special bird in the form of a carving, a photograph, or a painting. Because Emi was such an avid reader who consumed books at the rate of one every two days, I always included a number of books concealed in elegant gift wrap, chosen from her yearly book wish list, which she was only too happy to share with me. I concluded with a gift designed to keep Emi warm during the winter: fuzzy socks, thick gloves, or a fleecy cardigan. In addition, her solstice stocking hanging from the mantel always contained a tiny bear or eagle fetish carved in beautiful stone, followed by dark chocolates of all kinds, festively covered in red, silver, or gold foil, finally ending with one traditional tangerine in the toe to soften the sugar guilt.

On her part, Emi, who mail-ordered most of her presents, consistently showered me with fabulous gifts: gold and diamond jewelry, silk clothing, books about bird identification or Native American culture and beliefs, Zuni fetishes, and miniature horse reproductions from the Trail of the Painted Ponies. My stocking always contained a lead figure or two, which Emi had personally painted and signed, several hair barrettes she created in loom beading featuring Native American designs, a silver pendant and chain, a special bookmark, and that traditional, obligatory tangerine!

After our showers Emi and I spent the day until dinner reading our new books, sometimes to each other, while wearing our new clothing items, and enjoying the warmth of a cheerful fire and hot chocolate. "Darling," Emi exclaimed happily, on the rare occasion she could lift her eyes from a new mystery, "this book is excellent and so interesting! I'll never figure out which character committed the murder!" And back she would go, nose in the book until it was time to prepare dinner, a feast which always included two, thick Porterhouse steaks that we grilled rare for Emi and medium rare for me. We traditionally ended the meal with chocolate ice cream drenched in chocolate sauce, topped with whipped cream and a cherry to satisfy Emi's chocolate-craving sweet tooth!

As it grew dark outside, on this longest night of the year, Emi and I laid a slender mattress, covered with a soft, furry blanket and two pillows, on the carpet in front of the fireplace. Once the fire had morphed magically into glowing embers, we turned out all of the lights except for the tree and lay before the fireplace in nothing but our silk robes. We ended this wondrous celebration the way it had begun, making slow, passionate love and lying in each other's arms afterwards, basking in the red glow and warmth of the soft firelight until our drooping eyes and tired bodies summoned us to bed. We repeated our love celebration every Winter Solstice this same way except, of course, that our love became richer and truer as we aged.

The first Winter Solstice after I lost Emi occurred only a few months after her death when my feelings were still on the edge of raw, and every memory was salt in the wound. I spent much of that day in the basement, wailing uncontrollably at the stark reality of my devastating loss. There were no lights, no tree, no gifts, no food, and no fire. The dark fireplace was as empty as my heart. Appropriately, it was an overcast day that just deepened into black as time wore on. Indeed, I felt, this was the longest, cruelest night of the year.

Elizabeth Kidwell

When I awoke the next morning, following a fitful few hours of sad, restless sleep, I felt a deep hunger inside of me, but it wasn't for food. In my desperate, troubled mind, I believed that the only people who could help me survive my loss or even understand what I was going through were other lesbians who had also suffered the death of their partners. I began to search the Internet for older women support groups in Indianapolis: nothing. Even Ellen, my grief therapist, could not suggest one because they just did not exist. It seemed to me that other lesbians must be stronger than I was and didn't need the support of strangers to recover from their losses.

Fortunately, my sister Louise had invited me to fly to California to spend Christmas and New Year's with her family, so I already had my ticket to Oakland for a late-morning flight. Suddenly, it dawned on me. I would be spending the next three weeks in the Bay Area only one hour's drive from San Francisco. San Francisco, the lesbian and gay capital of the world! I thought, surely, there would be a support group there. I turned to Safari once more, and sure enough! My heart suddenly flipped inside my chest. There it was: an older lesbian support group that met at a Jewish community outreach center in San Francisco. I was saved! How I longed for this meeting! I was packed and ready when Ann arrived to take me to the airport. I boarded the airplane, although with the sudden lightness of hope in my heart, I felt that I could have flown to California on my own wings!

When my sister Louise picked me up at the Oakland Airport at noon, her wide eyes at first registered alarm. I had lost fifty pounds since she last saw me in October, but she made no comment. As soon as we climbed into her van for the ride home, I told her about the meeting in San Francisco and my plan. Later that afternoon, tender-hearted Louise researched the Internet for the telephone number of the Jewish center hosting the support group. She called the center and spoke briefly with the receptionist about the meeting, thanked the woman, and hung up with a frown. She turned to me slowly with the bad news and said, "The group use to meet there, but they stopped coming over a year ago. It's an old website that was never taken down." At her words, the tiny flame of hope winked out in my chest, and my face fell. Louise looked concerned at my transformation. "I'll find something," she promised, determination hardening her resolve. Hours later, she finally gave up her search, having only discovered a lesbian meet-up for twenty and thirty year olds for that night in nearby San Leandro. Louise offered to drive me, but at sixty-five, I declined to go. I wasn't searching for romance, just for relief from this incessant pain that dominated my life.

By late afternoon, I had situated myself at the far end of the dining room table. Books, writing supplies, and my iPad sat before me, creating my little security nook, and that is where I spent most of the next three weeks. Often during the day, Louise would sit next to me at the table with her own iPad, occasionally speaking, but mostly just being there quietly for me, a companion in my grief until she left to pick up the kids. When my niece Caroline and nephew Joseph arrived home from school that first day, I hugged them warmly, but when I started crying, I could tell that they felt uncomfortable and did not know what to say to me. So as soon as politely possible, they vanished upstairs to do homework they didn't have. My brother-in-law Eugene was equally sweet when he came home from work a short time later. He kindly expressed his sadness for my loss of Emi as tears rolled down my cheeks.

Later that same evening after Eugene and the kids had retired for the night, Louise and I sat in the living room watching television. Hitting the mute button, Louise turned to me and said, "When I flew to Indiana last fall, Eugene could not understand why I had to make the trip twice. After seeing you today, he told me that he understood. I am sorry that we could not find any help for you, Ellie." My only response to her were the silent tears trickling from my eyes.

The next morning after Eugene left for work, dropping the kids off at school Christmas parties on his way, Louise and I sat drinking coffee in the dining room. "Have you ever read the book, *The Year of Magical Thinking* by Joan Didion?" Louise asked.

"No," I responded. "What is it about?"

"It is a book she wrote following the death of her husband in 2003. I thought it might help you to read it," she explained. "Let's go to the library this morning and see if they have it."

Elizabeth Kidwell

The San Leandro Public Library indeed had a copy, and Louise checked it out for me, placing the small memoir in my hands. Arriving home, I took my spot at the dining room table and began to read, blocking out everything else around me. Joan Didion had lost her husband and writing partner, John Gregory Dunne, to an unexpected massive heart attack at their dinner table on December 30, 2003. As I read deeper into the book, I entered Joan's grief world while already heavily burdened with my own. Attempting to be objective and analytical, Joan's magical thinking paralleled my own. We both replayed in our minds the deaths of our loved ones over and over in an attempt to discover if we could have affected a different outcome had we noticed the possibility of impending tragedy in advance. If we had been more aware, more loving, more careful, could we have we have turned Death away? At times, however, Joan Didion's experience of the derangement of grief was intensely personal and mirrored my own sorrowful insanity. Yes, I thought, finishing the book that evening, Joan Didion was a fellow grief zombie.

The next day Louise took me last minute Christmas shopping with her. She believed that the fresh air and a change of place would be good for me. The San Leandro Costco was packed with last minute shoppers, but the crowd did not deter us. We squeezed up each aisle until we were lucky enough to find large packages of turkey and beef jerky, along with huge boxes of Pop Tarts for Eugene's sister's family, annual gifts that I never understood until Christmas morning when I watched Eugene's teenaged niece and nephews tear into them, a strange combination that they actually loved!

I would imagine that to most people, Emi and I had been a strange combination, too. She was like beef jerky, fire-hardened, tough, resilient, and salty. I, on the other hand, was like a Pop Tart, heat-softened, sugar-coated, crumbly, and sweet. Somewhat magically, our blended lives worked, most of all, I believe, because Emi carried within herself, a secret softness. The first movie we saw together was *Gorillas in the Mist*, a 1988 biopic of wildlife expert Dian Fossey, portrayed by Sigourney Weaver. The ending of the film was emotional to say the least, but I was more touched to discover Emi sobbing into her handkerchief next to me. When I asked if she was all right, Emi looked at me with her red, swollen eyes and said, "Don't ever tell anyone about this, or it will ruin my reputation."

After that first time, Emi cried at every movie we ever saw. Instinctively, I began to stuff wads of Kleenex into my pockets, and from then on we rated each film's effectiveness by counting the number of tissues Emi used to staunch the flow of tears. Her personal best was a five hanky cry over the movie *Marley and Me* in 2008, despite the fact that she had read the book several times before we went to see it. I kept her secret as she requested throughout our lives together. However, it didn't take movies to make me cry. It only took my great love for Emi in the aftermath of her loss. Everything.

Elizabeth Kidwell

How fitting it is that I celebrate
the longest night and darkest day
of the year without you, my love.
I am on a downward spiral of grief
today as I remember how bright
Solstice once was when we two lay
by the fireplace intertwined in warmth
and each other. It did not matter
how dark it became then because
we each carried the flame of love
hot for each other. The white glow
of the fire illuminated our bodies
with soft, flickering light, our minds
lit too, where love really lives, and
the greatest gifts we gave were
ourselves, totally, completely, and
delightedly One. So what do I give
you now from this dark and cold place
I one time called my heart? What do
I wrap for you when you are no longer
able to thank me? Enveloped as I am
in sorrow, I make a poor gift this year.
You are not even here to open me
and act surprised at the love beaming back at
you, but it is all still here, just as blazing as
ever in my memory where I see you
constantly. How can I let go of you,
the gift you gave me over and over with love?

Wounded Wings

And how can I ever deny the person
I was in your presence? Even the sun
turns away at that prospect this winter.
Still, its rays shine brightest on blue days
And gradually lighten this troubled time.

Chapter 17
Breath

Emi's mother Marie died in her sleep when she was sixty-nine, just one year after Raymond, Emi's father, died at the age of seventy-two. Emi was in the habit of calling Marie from school in the late morning to check up on her. That particular morning, however, Marie did not answer the phone. Concerned, Emi called her close friend Eva, who had a key to Marie's house, and asked her to drive over and check on her mother. Eva found Marie unmoving, still in bed in a fetal position, wrapped in blankets, her little dog, ever faithful, at her side. The dog growled in warning and would not allow her to touch Marie, so Eva phoned Emi back. "I think you'd better get over here as soon as you can. Your mother doesn't appear to be breathing and she wouldn't answer when I called her name. Euglena is growling and won't let me near enough to check."

A half hour later, Emi arrived at her mother's house, removed the dog, and checked for a pulse. Nothing. Emi turned to Eva, who loved Marie almost as much as she did, and apologized, "I am so sorry that you had to be the one to find her. I know how much you loved her, too." It was the saddest day of Emi's life to that point because there was no one besides Beth who held her love and life so closely.

From that moment on, Emi believed that she would die in her sleep at the age of sixty-nine just like her mother, and she wanted to be prepared. Now truly an orphan, she called her attorney to make out a will, which she found necessary to update about every five years after that to reflect the gradual changes in her life as she continued to live longer. Years later, following Beth's death, Emi drew up a new will, and five years after that, she met me.

From our very beginning, Emi would lecture me on the importance of being prepared for the inevitable eventuality of death, often making it sound like the crowning moment of life, an event to look out for. So I too retained a lawyer, who drew up my own last will and testament and a power of attorney, appointing Emi as executor and POA, as she did for me. Now, I believed, we could get on with the business of living, but always gnawing in the back of my mind, was the specter of Emi dying in her sleep.

One Saturday morning when Emi was sixty-eight, I descended the stairs at her house and walked softly into her bedroom to see if she was awake yet. I was usually met with the sound of regular soft breathing or gentle snoring, but this morning I heard no sound coming from her bed. Fearfully, I approached Emi and leaned over. No sound came from her nose or her mouth. I could just make out her chest in the grey morning light. It was not rising and falling. Silently, I placed my hand in front of her face and detected no breath! Convinced the worst had occurred, I instantly burst into tears, and unbidden, set up a full-scale wailing, loud and mournful. Hearing my cries, Emi's eyes flew open in alarm. "Bunting, what's wrong?" she asked, deep concern suddenly etched on her face.

Through my tears, I managed to blurt out, "I thought you had died in your sleep!"

"Oh dear!" Emi responded, lifting her bedcovers, inviting me inside. I crawled in sniffling and shivering, but not from cold. "Darling," she continued to comfort me, "I am all right. See? I am so sorry I gave you a fright, but you gave me one, too!" She grabbed a few Kleenex from the box on her bedside table and gave them to me. "You are a liquid mess," she observed, as she dabbed my tear-stained face. Then she pulled me close and warmed me lovingly until I calmed down. "You know," she began, after I was the one breathing normally once again, "You have given me an idea of what it will be like around here when I really die, and it won't be pretty!" Then with a wink and a grin, she teased me. "I am just glad that I won't be around when this happens for real!" I barely managed a smile. Then, comfortingly, we made sweet love, and I eventually recovered from the shock I had suffered. But from then on, Emi would periodically rib me about my wail-fest, trying to make me feel better about the inevitable end of my happy world. Much to her surprise, Emi did not die at sixty-nine, so we continued to delight in each other as we welcomed new adventures to places we had never seen.

Elizabeth Kidwell

Emi loved Lake Michigan, and I loved lighthouses. Combining the two, we planned a three-week journey around the lake during the summer of 1992, culminating in a one-week stay on the peninsula of Door County, Wisconsin. For the first two weeks, we did a lighthouse tour along the east shore, exploring and photographing as many lighthouses as possible. Beginning with Grand Haven, we also collected Little Sable Point, Ludington North Pierhead, Big Sable Point, Manistee North Pierhead, Old Mission Point, Grand Traverse, North Manitou, and the Straits of Mackinac lighthouses. Of course, Emi had to take a photo of me in front of every lighthouse we visited. We continued on around to the western shore of Lake Michigan, crossing over the Upper Peninsula into Wisconsin, and ending up on beautiful Door County, a finger of land pointing out into the lake. We had booked a lovely motel room in Egg Harbor, making daily trips to Newport State Park for afternoon picnics and strolls on the beach. It was early August, and Door County's harvests of red raspberries and sweet cherries were at their peak. Since we were both berry/cherry lovers, we bought a fresh basket of each daily from a small stand sitting by the side of the road that led to the park.

That first day at Newport, we chose a picnic table shaded by a large tree and enjoyed our gourmet lunch. It wasn't long before a thirteen-line ground squirrel or "squinney" scurried up to beg for food. I was charmed by the alternating brown, white, and dotted stripes running lengthwise along his back, and I immediately named him Stripey. Before long, after sampling all the food in our basket, he developed a preference for red raspberries, although they were not one of his diet staples. I became so fond of Stripey, that I insisted we take our lunch at the same table for the rest of our stay. Sure enough, every afternoon, as soon as we unpacked our basket lunch, Stripey appeared, eventually climbing up on my bench. Sitting politely next to me, he accepted only the food I handed to him, usually red raspberries, once I realized that he preferred them. His tiny paws grasped each berry, touching my fingers softly, delicately. Emi and I grew fond of the little creature, and after that, it just wasn't a picnic without Stripey. Emi loved nature as much as I did, but my relationship with Stripey greatly amused her. Like clockwork, he joined us each day. On our last day on Door County, we were happily strolling arm and arm along the beach when we came upon an appalling sight. Before us lay hundreds of dead, decaying fish washed up on the shore. Always the biologist, Emi explained that this was called Summer Kill, which occurred when the lake water warmed up during the day and water plants consumed too much oxygen in the morning just at dawn. "Unfortunately," she told me, "the fish often do not sense the danger and fail to swim out of area in time. They die from oxygen starvation and wash up on the beach, gasping for breath."

Later that day, Emi and I drove to the picnic area and commandeered our usual table. We set out the tablecloth, plates, and food, but Stripey was curiously absent. As we began our meal, I expressed concern for my little friend. "I hope nothing has happened to Stripey," I said, wrinkles of worry gathering on my face. We were almost finished with our picnic when Stripey finally made his appearance and scampered up next to me.

As I began to feed him, Emi breathed a sigh of relief and blurted out the words that would become our humorous cry of thanksgiving whenever one of us was late getting home to the other for the rest of our days together, "Stripey, thank God!"

That last night in Egg Harbor, I awoke uncharacteristically around midnight and heard nothing. Dead silence. I decided not to panic this time and sat on the edge of my bed, listening for Emi just two feet away. After some time that seemed like forever to me, Emi sputtered to life and began to breathe. Relieved, I thought to sleep again when I became aware that Emi's breathing had once more stopped. I grabbed my Timex Indiglo watch off the bedside table and clocked the silence. Twenty seconds later, Emi snorted and continued breathing. Snoring mildly for the next forty seconds, she suddenly grew silent again. There would be no sleep for me now! I was wide awake and continued to time Emi for the next fifteen minutes before lying down and sleeping fitfully the rest of the night, unsettled by what I had discovered.

In the morning Emi awoke first and climbed into bed with me. I opened my eyes, pleasantly awakened by the warmth of her body snuggling against me and her sweet smile, greeting me like the rising sun. Neither of us wanted to pack. Our vacation seemed so perfect, so relaxing, so loving, and both of us agreed that if our lives continued like this, it would feel like heaven on earth. Wisely, realistically, we understood only too well that the only constant in our lives was change. So we began to pack for the drive home.

It was after breakfast that I decided to share with Emi what I had discovered. "I woke up last night and you weren't breathing again," I began. Emi's eyes connected with mine registering curiosity. "I timed you," I explained. "Out of every minute, you stopped breathing for twenty seconds. I think that when we arrive home, we need to see the doctor. This might explain why you have been so tired lately."

"I agree with you, Darling," Emi responded, concern showing in her face. "We will."

Back in Indianapolis, the outcome of that doctor appointment led to a sleep study, and soon Emi was diagnosed with sleep apnea. She took the news in stride as another bump in the road of life, and soon she was peacefully sleeping or napping with her CPAP as if she was born to it. Best of all, her energy increased and so did the number of life adventures we shared. Five years later, I too was diagnosed with sleep apnea when I began to fall asleep at strange times during the day. So CPAP use became just one more thing we shared and two more items to pack before a trip. Nothing slowed us down!

It was 1995, the year following my cancer surgery and the year before Emi was diagnosed with breast cancer. Emi and I were visiting our nearby public library as we frequently did on Saturday afternoons. While Emi was in the mystery section selecting a half-dozen mysteries to keep her supplied for the following week, I was browsing the book shelf that featured new arrivals. There before me was the latest winner of the National Book Award: *How We Die: Reflections on Life's Final Chapter* by Sherwin B. Nuland, M.D. Dr. Nuland was the Clinical Professor of Surgery at Yale University, and he was also a finalist for the Pulitzer Prize.

Curious, I immediately checked out his book, and for the next three weeks, I was mystified by the beautiful prose Dr. Nuland used to explain the experience of leaving life. I read slowly each evening, absorbing the frank and realistic explanation of what really happens when people die. I was especially heartened when Dr. Nuland explained that our intellectual capacities such as reasoning and judgment are quite often unimpaired until late in life. Dying, he concluded, is a process in which every tissue of the body participates over time toward the taking of that last breath.

The knowledge I gained from this book helped me in the years to come as Emi aged and physically began to change and to fail. Most helpful was the advice Dr. Nuland gave about the last days of life. The family and the patient, he insisted, not the doctors and the hospital, should determine how the last remaining days will be lived out. By the time Emi left this world, seventeen years later, that is exactly how she and I planned our last decisions and lived our final hours together. When Emi finally took her last breath, I did not embarrass her at the hospital. I wanted her passing to be peaceful and dignified so I suffered the shock in silence. Even my drive home was safety silent, but as soon as entered the front door, I lost it. Crawling weakly into Emi's empty bed, I gave voice to my broken heart. Emi was right. It was a good thing that she wasn't around to hear it.

Elizabeth Kidwell

Once, when you stopped breathing in sleep,
I stood over your bed in a dark dawn,
Thinking you had died
And set up such a wailing
That startled, you awoke
Surprised to find me mourning you.

"Darling, what is it?"
You asked,
As tender tears enveloped you.

Without hesitation,
You lifted the covers
And pulled me into your
Warm softness
To prove
That you were very much alive.

Years later, on the day
You actually died,
I had to be the brave one.
Selfishly, I wanted to keep you
Until the last minute
Loving me, though you would suffer

The pain of leaving, but instead
I chose to ease your struggle
Letting you slip peacefully, painlessly away.
Did you know that I was there,
Endless hours, a sad sentinel,
Holding your hand
Through each ragged breath

Wounded Wings

That lanced my life in two?

And then in endless soaring,
Your spirit took its flight.
Still, you have a home within me
Whenever you choose to land,
Where just the very thought of you
Will always take my breath away.

Chapter 18
Clothed

One of the necessary chores that Emi disliked, especially as she grew older, was shopping for clothes. After she retired from teaching, she kept her wardrobe simple to reflect her casual lifestyle. Her everyday attire usually consisted of outdoor wear: jeans or walking shorts, a T-shirt, and a colorful, patterned, long-sleeved over shirt. She added cotton socks and comfortable walking shoes, or hiking boots if we went birdwatching, a pastime we delighted in at least once a week. During the winter, she changed to wool socks and flannel shirts, cardigans, or pull over sweaters, and flannel-lined jeans. Rather than subject herself to store shopping, she kept catalogues and ordered most of her clothing over the phone from companies such as Land's End, Travel Smith, or L.L. Bean. When her packages arrived, it always felt like Christmas as she opened them to display her new duds!

As Emi aged, we made several adjustment to her undergarments. When she developed incontinence, she exchanged panties for senior pull-ups without the slightest problem or embarrassment. If discreet senior undergarments would allow her the freedom of continued traveling, adventuring, and birdwatching, the adaptation was totally worth it as far as she was concerned. I was more than pleased with her for welcoming this transition in her life as if it was the most natural thing to do! So I proudly added Depends to my weekly shopping list from then on. Handing her the packages, I teased her lovingly, and privately called her "my diaper dandy!" Then there was the arthritis that developed in her shoulders during her seventies, and wearing a bra became as she described it, "penitential." She had no problem giving up bras, although she made concessions for special dress up occasions.

During her late seventies, footwear became a problem also. I noticed that Emi began to buy new shoes almost once a month, expensive shoes that she would wear for a while and then discard in her closet after shopping for a more comfortable replacement pair. Eventually, the wearing of shoes and even socks became impossible as the pain and numbness in her feet increased. Emi began to go barefoot in the house until the arches of her feet began to fall, adding even more pain to walking. After a visit to her neurologist, Emi was diagnosed with neuropathy of the feet, although she had never been diabetic. Strong medication eased the pain somewhat, and following a visit to her podiatrist, she was fitted with orthotics as well. Happily, we discovered while attending a Native American pow-wow that she could tolerate wearing moccasins with her orthotic inserts whenever she needed to walk, and we purchased three pair. Sadly, however, hikes and birdwatching on foot became out of the question. Eventually, the neuropathy traveled up her legs, and for a while, she could not tolerate the wearing of jeans or slacks, but the neurologist found a medication for that condition, too, and we were back in the traveling business once again! Emi met every setback with a stride forward as we created adaptations to our lifestyle. The expensive, unworn shoes were donated to a church-sponsored organization, which provided used clothing and footwear to several African outreach groups.

"When I die," Emi used to tell me once she reached the age of eighty, "I want you to donate my clothing right away to Thrifty Threads. Don't wait. The money they make selling donated clothing goes to battered women shelters in the city."

Choking back the specter of predictable sadness, I promised her that I would, although as I was to discover, it would be more difficult than she made it sound.

Four months after Emi died, I was feeling particularly strong one day, and decided to fulfill the promise I had made to her. It took me a week to complete this project, not because Emi owned so many clothes, but because the memories slowed me down. Practically every piece of her clothing carried with it at least one poignant memory of happier times.

Bravely, I began my project in the coat closet opposite the front door of the house, where every jacket, coat, hat, pair of gloves, and scarf that Emi had ever worn, hung silently, just waiting for me. The last time this closet door had been opened was by my sister Louise in October 2012. She was visiting for the second time, planning and organizing Emi's memorial open house, and to keep me busy, she suggested that I clean this closet out so that guests would have a place to hang their coats. When she opened the closet door for me, I took one look and immediately burst into tears! Shaken by my strong response, Louise quickly shut the door and gave up on that idea, realizing how hopeless I truly was. So it was that our guests had to lay their jackets and coats on Emi's bed.

    I now faced the task on my own in this silent house. It was early December and I encouragingly convinced myself that many homeless people would need her outerwear to keep warm this coming winter. I selected the first shirt hanging on the left, a heavy, Army-green, long-sleeved over shirt that Emi customarily wore during our spring birding trips. The memories that deluged my brain overwhelmed me, and I had to sit down to catch my breath. I collapsed onto a nearby stuffed chair in the living room, and holding the shirt lovingly on my lap, I let the memories wash over me. Suddenly, there we were, standing on the trail next to the lake at Eagle Creek Park, as we had so many times before, spotting, studying, and identifying rafts of migrating ducks using our spotting scope. There we were again, watching an osprey swoop down over the water to snag a fish in both talons and then rise into the air, the prized meal clamped securely. On later trips, we enjoyed the sight of a pair of bald eagles perched in the same tree, and felt the cool downdraft of two mute swans, just taking off from the water as they flew low overhead, so close that we could almost reach up and touch them. Another memory, and we were in Shades Park, hiking through the forest, but froze in place as twin, speckled white-tailed fawns chased each other in play around a tree. We watched delighted, blessed by a playtime spectacle that people seldom see. Sometime later, memories fading, I blew my nose, wiped my eyes, folded the shirt, and placed it gently into a large, paper shopping bag. One.

    Next, I selected the lightweight tan jacket that Emi habitually wore in the fall. Once again I sat down on a living room chair, touching the slick cotton weave softly. Unbidden, our life together came flooding back. Now, we were on our first trip to the Brookville Reservoir near Brookville, Indiana, where Emi had begun her teaching career at the high school so many decades ago. The trees surrounding the lake were brilliantly clothed in fall finery, and I understood then why Emi had fallen in love with this place, and her first adult home. Other memory pictures followed: standing arm-in-arm at the Falls of the Ohio careful not to slip on the wet limestone, viewing the breathtaking Clifty Falls, and delighting in beautiful Cataract Falls, the largest in Indiana, often delighting in the cool spray on our faces. Then, there was that fall break visit to Cumberland Gap Historical Park where we stood simultaneously in the states of Kentucky, Tennessee, and Virginia, while viewing together the first great pioneer gateway to the west. Once again, as these memories subsided, I folded the jacket and placed it in the bag on top of the green shirt. Two.

So it continued, a slow process for me. I didn't fare any better with her purple down winter jacket and her white silk neck scarf. There were more than twenty-five memories attached including shoveling snow off the driveway, then warming ourselves with steaming mugs of hot chocolate; engaging playfully in snowball fights; tramping arm in arm through gentle, falling snow; and enjoying those cold picnics in winter! Then there was that wondrous trip to Alaska and to the Pribilof Islands, discovering fantastic birds like red-faced cormorants, red-legged kittiwakes, thick-billed murres, horned and tufted puffins, and least and crested auklets. We stood holding hands while we gazed in wonder at the rocky beach below us where hundreds of Northern fur seals hauled out to breed. All these memories popped to life in my mind's eye once again. As they faded, I folded the bulky jacket and stuffed it into the sack. Three. And so it continued.

The flood of memories continued in her bedroom closet where her pantsuits and dresses reminded me of special occasions when Emi, as she described it, "put on the Ritz" for her famous birthday open houses or for the wedding of a dear friend when she was asked to be the honorary grandmother. I also winced tearfully when I began to clear out her dresser drawers. Her everyday clothes were even more precious in their memories of our daily life together, joyful and loving, and sometimes a little painful. Surprisingly to me, even missing clothing carried memories. One example that stood out in my mind was Emi's favorite yellow night shirt with black sheep all over it. She was wearing it the night I called an ambulance to take her to the emergency room at St. Vincent's Hospital. The sleepwear was inadvertently left behind when she was admitted to a room to be treated for cellulitis, wearing only a tasteless hospital gown. A week later, proud of being the black sheep of her family, although I always thought of her as her family's crowning glory, she mourned the loss of that simple piece of clothing. Now years later, gazing at her sad, empty drawer and closets, I mourned the loss of her with bitter tears. Finally, I had to remind myself again that I had photos of most of our adventures, and I did not need her clothing to remember them. Those memories of unforgettable life blessings were forever etched in my heart and mind.

Early on during my grief therapy, Ellen shared with me that some grieving people become so lonely that they feel a need to wear some of their loved-ones' clothing for comfort. During one of my daily crying jags, I tried on one of Emi's shirts, figuring I had nothing to lose, and while it felt a little like she was hugging me warmly, I realized that the memories consisted of her body in this clothing, not mine. I finally admitted to myself that I had to let her clothing go so other people could have the use of them. It was what Emi had wanted. A few days later, I loaded my car with all of her clothing and drove to Thrifty Threads. The workers there were delighted to receive her gift!

In the end I understood that I had never invited these memories to come; I just couldn't prevent them. Our lives together had been so rich, so adventuresome, so loving that my mind housed every special moment like treasure in my chest. I am a very wealthy woman, I realized, as I returned home from the thrift store in my empty car. Emi and I had created priceless memories during our lives together. While the strangers who would eventually wear Emi's clothes could never know these stories, I prayed that perhaps they would sense the warmth and the love she had possessed, and somehow be comforted and blessed.

Wounded Wings

Letting go of your clothing today
Did not cause me anguish and pain
Because when I think of covering,
I remember how my love and my body
Kept you much warmer than any coat,
How my arms wound around you
Securely, like loving gift wrap,
Surrounding you in protective care
More than any shirt or pants could do.
How I kissed the top of your head,
Warming your scalp of thinning hair
Better than any wool cap or hat.

We never used clothing to hide
Ourselves from the other because
Openness precluded clothes,
Making yours unnecessary even now
When I must move on without you.
In the spirit world you need nothing

But pure love and boundless understanding.
So I give your clothes to earth-bound spirits,
Who may not feel free to share themselves
With others without fear or embarrassment.
You are forever arrayed in the beauty of my love
In gratitude for all you are and were.
Always you clothed me in the greatest finery
You had to give: your bright, eternal love.

Chapter 19
General

Emi and I spent a good part of our first few years together visiting state parks in both Indiana and Kentucky, usually on weekends. We would stay either in the park lodge or in a secluded cabin in the woods. Emi's favorite Indiana state park was Turkey Run, where she had spent every summer of her childhood during the 1930's. Her parents, both science teachers, took summer jobs as naturalists at Turkey Run, and the family had lived in one of the rustic cabins along Trail 6. This trail also led to Sugar Creek, where Emi enjoyed the freedom to play all summer long, surrounded by nature, discovering plants, trees, creek creatures, and a large variety of birds, snakes, and woodland mammals. During their first summer at Turkey Run, Emi's parents took in an abandoned flying squirrel named Freddy to raise, so they dubbed their cabin The Squirrel House. Eventually, they provided a home for baby raccoons and fox squirrels, too, and Emi came to regard them as surrogate brothers and sisters! Emi's father Raymond taught her all about birds, instilling in her a lifelong passion for birdwatching and an endless quest to add more birds to her life list. When Emi began to adopt baby snakes, her dad taught her the difference between venomous and nonvenomous species to keep her safe. Emi's mother Marie, a botanist, taught her everything she knew about plants and trees, including which ones were poisonous. Armed with this knowledge, Emi was granted the freedom of exploring both Turkey Run and Sugar Creeks along Trail 6, and little by little, a trail-blazing scientist and nature lover was born!

One Friday afternoon in late spring, ten months after we became life partners, I arrived home from school early to find Emi there waiting for me. She greeted me at my front door curiously excited about something. Grinning broadly, she explained that she was going to kidnap me for the weekend and take me across state lines on a mystery trip! "Where?" was the first question out of my mouth.

"Well," teased Emi, "if I told you, it wouldn't be a surprise, would it? You'll see soon enough. Go get packed for the weekend, and include outdoor clothing and a swimsuit. Park your car in the garage. I'm driving."

"We're leaving now?" I asked, a pleased smile on my face.

"Yes," she grinned, "and don't bring along any school work."

Soon we were happily driving south on I 65, singing together most of the way. We turned off toward Madison, Indiana, crossing the bridge over the Ohio River into Kentucky. Soon we arrived at General Butler State Resort Park in Carrollton, where Emi had secured reservations at the Hilltop Lodge. The drive had taken only two hours, and it was still daylight. After unpacking, Emi treated me to a delicious dinner at the Two Rivers Restaurant.

The weekend was glorious! We hiked, identified spring warblers, and rowed a canoe on the lake. Exhausted, Emi took her customary afternoon nap while I read, and when she awoke, we made love until dinner time, the afternoon sun warming us from a high window. We spent the evenings stargazing, sitting by the fire in the lobby, or snuggling together on the sofa in our room. Everything was perfect, and when we returned home Sunday evening, we were both rested and revitalized because of our special time together.

One evening a year later, Emi arrived at my house on Tuesday night, our once-a-week "video night" we called it, although I didn't own a video player, and neither of us watched much television. Emi met me at the door with a somber look on her face, and immediately, I knew that something serious had occurred. "Emi, what's wrong?" I questioned her. I was instantly alarmed by the serious look in her eyes.

Emi sat me down on the sofa in my living room. Then facing me and taking my hands in her own, using a tone of voice I had never heard before, she told me. "Army intelligence has intercepted information that there is a contract on my life. It appears to exist in retaliation for work I had done on one of my missions."

"What does that mean?" I asked, fear gripping my heart like an icy, metallic vice.

Seeing the fear on my face, Emi continued. There was absolutely no way to sugar coat the danger she faced. "Darling, protective measures for me are already in place. There is a tap on my phone, and it will be monitored 24/7. My protectors are housed in a home nearby where they can have a clear view of my house day and night. In addition, I will have a protective detail following me wherever I go."

At her words, I at first felt a sense of relief, immediately followed by a strong feeling of alarm. Once again, I felt like I was living in an espionage film with all its inherent dangers. How can all this be true, I wondered, when we live such simple lives? My mind was spinning in confusion, and once again, I began to doubt Emi's sanity, and then my own. I was speechless.

But she wasn't living a simple life, I knew. Whenever I traveled to California to visit my family or whenever she went off for weeks at a time to Elderhostels without me, there were missions she completed about which I knew nothing. Of course, I theorized, much of her service was dangerous, involving ruthless people. She was far from being retired from intelligence work. I was the one who lived the plain, simple life of loving a highly-regarded spy.

When I lifted my face and looked deeply into Emi's eyes, I discovered more serious concern. "Bunting," she continued, as if all she had already told me was not enough. "There is more." I sucked in air and held my breath, wondering how much worse it could get and dreading to hear more. "I told them," she continued, "that I don't want their protection if they cannot protect you, too." It took me a few moments to process the meaning of what she had just told me. "So," she continued, "they agreed to protect you also."

Sometimes, I felt like a fugitive in my beloved country of freedom and equality. Emi and I were married to each other in every sense of the word but legal. Same sex marriages sanctioned by the Supreme Court were years away. Had we been legally married, there would have been no question of protecting Emi's spouse. As valuable and important as she was to the intelligence community, her rank already equivalent to a highly decorated army colonel, I was later to discover, she should never have had to ask.

I went numb inside, but before I could ask the question, she answered it for me. "No, you will never see them, but they will be guarding us both."

"For how long?" I managed to blurt out in my shock, my mind spinning like a metal top.

"There is no way to know," Emi responded, as she leaned over to envelop me in her strong arms. "It could be weeks, months, or even years. There is no way to predict, but they will inform me when the danger has passed."

"I am so scared for you!" I cried, bursting into tears. At that, Emi held me tenderly and lovingly, but it was a long time before I stopped crying. As it turned out, it was a very long time before the threat was over, too, years in fact.

At one point, I thought I knew where our guardians were housed. On the next street to the east of us, the owners of a two-story house curiously installed a huge picture window with no curtains upstairs at the back of the of the house. I glanced up at that window often, and while the window afforded the large room plenty of natural light, I never saw anyone in that room during the day, and at night, there were never any lights burning. The only view it afforded was an unobstructed one of the front of Emi's house and the street. I theorized that the room contained cameras monitored from another room. Occasionally, I would drive by the front of that house, which always looked well cared for, but I never saw anyone outside, unlike the other houses on the block teaming with families and children, and curiously, the curtains were always drawn.

If Emi was concerned about the contract on her life, she never showed it. She remained her sweet, funny self, always moving forward in her pursuit of wonders. I wish I could say that I was as brave as she was. For Emi's sake, I put on a good front, pretending that this terrifying threat never entered my thoughts, but in reality, there it was, gnawing at my brain every time life afforded me a chance to catch my breath. The very real threat that this incredible woman could be taken from me at any time, kept me on edge most days. Eventually, however, as our love deepened and matured, I learned to cherish even more our days together, trying as hard as I could to keep the image of the threat from my daily thoughts and to focus my heart on my sweet companion and our fantastic life. In a very real sense, I understood the fear that the spouses of police officers, fire-fighters, and military personnel contend with every day, and I tried to live as bravely as they did. I wasn't alone, I comforted myself. There are millions of us. On her part, Emi did her best to keep me distracted with continuous adventures.

One fall day, a couple of years later, Emi said to me, "Let's go see how General Butler State Resort Park looks in autumn. Want to?"

"Yes!" I responded, totally up for a break already, so early in the school year. "We had such a great time there the first time we visited in spring." This year, my fall break consisted of a four-day weekend, a teacher's dream, and Emi was surprisingly able to get reservations for a two-bedroom, secluded cottage due to a cancellation.

It was a glorious weekend with fabulous fall foliage, and Emi had another surprise for me. Shortly after we arrived, she gifted me with small silver star in a clear plastic box. "You have always been my shining star," she explained happily, holding my hand gently and placing the box into my palm. At that time, I did not realize the significance of this star. That understanding was to come much later.

Early that evening, Emi and I drove from our cottage to the Two Rivers Restaurant, a name that referred to the convergence of the Ohio and the Kentucky rivers, and the only eatery in the park. As we walked into the restaurant, my attention was drawn inexplicably to a solemn-faced, mature, solitary woman seated at a corner table toward the back of the dining hall on a slightly higher level. From that vantage point, I realized, she had a commanding view of the entire dining area, as she sat with her back to the corner wall behind her. Emi and were seated at a table with a lovely view, but I occasionally stole glances at the mysterious woman sitting alone at her table across the way on high ground. Emi and I ordered a delicious steak dinner and enjoyed our first evening at General Butler, the park named for a famous Kentucky general in the Revolutionary War.

Later, as we rose to leave, I noticed that the strange woman was still seated at her table. By the time Emi and I had reached the car, the woman was crossing the parking lot, too. As she passed us, Emi caught her eye and nodded. Wordlessly, looking at Emi, the woman lowered her head in greeting. After we were seated in the car, I asked Emi, "Who was that woman you just acknowledged?"

"Our protector," she answered in a whisper, but I never saw the woman again that weekend. A year later Emi broke the news to me that the danger had passed and we no longer needed protection.

A few weeks after Emi died, I visited her attorney's office in order to secure her box of service medals. I was ushered into the office of an assistant attorney, who handed me a letter signed by Emi. The letter informed me that I could not take possession of the box until six months after her death. Immediately, I felt hurt and confused. When Emi had told me that her medals were secure at her attorney's office, she made no mention of waiting six months. Returning home with nothing, my crying bouts continued, only this time, more bitterly. Why would Emi want to hurt me after she was dead, I wondered sadly.

Investigating further, I contacted a close friend of Emi's who had actually driven her to the attorney's office in back in 2003. Quickly, I recognized that this puzzling action on Emi's part had occurred after Emi fell and hit her head in 2003, followed by a period in which she acted suspiciously and trusted no one, obviously not even me. I consoled myself with the knowledge that she had not been herself at that time. She loved me, I knew, and would never willfully hurt me. She was protective of me and would have fought anyone who tried to cause me harm. So I waited the six months, secure in the belief that the medals were safe at the lawyer's office. I couldn't have been more wrong.

On February 27, 2013, I returned to the attorney's office and requested the box she had left for me. I waited alone in the office for at least thirty minutes, wondering why it was taking so long. When the lawyer returned, he carried only Emi's letter from before. He sat down at his desk, solemnly facing me and said the words that I dreaded to hear. "The box is not here."

"What do you mean?" I asked, raising my voice in alarm.

"I mean we can't locate the box anywhere in the files. Are you sure that someone didn't already pick it up?"

"Nine months ago, Emi herself told me that the box was here," I insisted, my voice now calm and level, my eyes fixed on his. "She had not been able to drive for over three years," I continued, "and the letter you hold in your hand names the only person you were to release it to, me."

"I don't know what to do," he responded. It was obvious from his tone that he was becoming frustrated by me.

"I suggest that you think outside the file. Surely your firm has at least one storage room," I suggested, stating the obvious. "Perhaps it is there."

"Maybe if you tell me what is in the box, that will help us find it," he suggested.

"I can't tell you what is in the box," I replied, "but I can tell you that its contents are priceless to me, and they are irreplaceable. The box is covered in light paper secured by twine, and my name and address are written on the outside," I explained, giving him the description that Emi's friend had given me. "I am leaving now, but I will call you every week to remind you until you find it." With that, I rose and left the office. Devastated, I cried all the way home. True to my word, I telephoned every week, and the answer was always the same. Eventually, the attorney told me that they had directed two secretaries to spend a day looking for the box, but to no avail. However, I got the feeling that they had given up, and after months passed, calling them became a useless activity for me because the box was hopelessly lost and there was nothing I could do. Alarmed, I came to worry that perhaps government intelligence had removed the medals from the attorneys' office without their knowledge, so that even in death, Emi would remain a "ghost." This concern caused me another bout of crying.

Meanwhile, having already worked on the house for a year, I continued to clear it out room by room though progress was slow, despite the fact that kind friends would stop by to help at least once a week. I had already sold the house, and the new owners were gracious enough to grant me an additional six months to complete the task. Yet so many of Emi's belongings and furniture had to be sold or auctioned, and I performed every task with a heavy heart. For twenty-five years, I had never looked into any of Emi's drawers, files, or closets. I just knew there was a lot of stuff. I had begun in the two-room basement. Clearing it out took months. Next, I moved up to the rooms of the ground floor, discovering surprising heirlooms day after day, including Emi's treasure-trove of old black and white photographs. Our life memories continued to side rail me, but I kept on room by room, ending with the garage.

Finally, after a year, I began to clear out the large guest bedroom closet upstairs. The closet contained a built-in chest of drawers, where Emi had stored more of her priceless belongings. When I opened the top drawer, it was packed with white boxes: dozens of small ones surrounding a single large one in the middle. Curiously, I could not remove the large box without removing the small boxes first. I soon discovered that the little boxes were filled with colored landscape slides of Emi's and Beth's numerous trips all over the world. In the thirty years they shared, they had traveled extensively and accumulated countless photos. There was no one, I knew, who would want these, and the two women who made these incredible memories together were gone. Sadly, I opened the boxes and dumped a lifetime of beautiful photographs in the trash. It felt like I was throwing Emi away.

It didn't take me long to discard the slides, and at last only the large, white box remained. As I worked to maneuver the box out of the drawer, I realized that it was quite heavy. "What could be in here?" I said aloud to myself. I set the box on my desk and lifted the lid. For a moment I stopped breathing! The familiar dark blue and gold cases I had first seen twenty-six years ago stared up at me, perfectly, neatly, and carefully arranged: Emi's missing medals! Naturally, tears began flowing once again, a combination of relief and pride. On two sheets of paper lying on top, Emi had carefully typed and printed off the names of every award and who had presented each one to her. She had entitled the list "She who has no name."

For over forty years, from the 1950's through the 1990's, Emi had served the country she loved with her whole heart, often putting her life on the line as any soldier would do. In fact, her decorations continued her legacy and described her loyal service: "exceptionally meritorious service to the government in a duty of great responsibility; exceptionally meritorious conduct in performance of outstanding service to the United States; singularly meritorious act of extraordinary fidelity; superior performance of duty; saving a life at the risk of one's own; courageous action in the line of duty; wounded in action seven times; valor and heroism, and distinctive defense service." Reading these words and holding her medals once again, I felt overwhelmed with love and respect for Emi. She was indeed a national hero, but she had been my hero first.

Curiously, the box also contained four unusual, enameled pins in the form of red, white, and blue shields, with one, two, three, or four stars. Doing online research, I discovered that they were pins worn on dress uniforms by an adjutant or an assistant to a one, two, three, and four star general respectively. I knew then that Emi had worn these symbols on her formal dress uniform when she was called to Washington, D.C., to take part in closed recognition ceremonies.

After I had opened all of Emi's cases and examined every decoration, only two insignia remained. On an army-green piece of stiff cardboard, Emi had mounted two silver eagles and two Silver Star pins, insignia she had never shared with me. Puzzled, I consulted the U.S. Army websites on the Internet. I learned that the silver eagle was the insignia of an Army colonel, and that she had worn them on the shoulders of her dress uniform. Finally, I turned my attention to the two silver stars. It took just moments to learn that these stars meant that Emi had been raised to the rank of a one-star or brigadier general before she had retired from her service in Army Intelligence. Suddenly, I understood the meaning of the Silver Star she had given me so many years ago! I had been the wife of a general!

Emi had never shared with me before that she held the rank of colonel and later, general. Perhaps she was not allowed to give out that information, or perhaps her devastating fall and resulting head injury in 2003 took away that memory. Whatever the reason for this omission, it was clear that after she somehow retrieved her medals from her attorney, Emi had left me a silent message. She knew that I would research the meaning of the insignia and be proud. She was never more right! My pride in her swelled my heart to bursting! How I loved this woman!

It was then that I glanced up at the small bookshelf where my therapy mandala sat, still incomplete, a hole in its center. There was no hesitation now, as I fully understood how to complete it. Placing the white box on the bed, I returned to my desk with a thick piece of art paper. Measuring the empty circle, I drew a quarter-sized circle. Carefully inside the circle, I drew a five-pointed star, using Emi's star as a model. I colored it using a silver pencil, and then cut it out. I secured the star inside the empty space with glue, and the mandala was finally complete! Emi's loss had left me with a hole in my center, but now I truly realized that to be the star of her life, I would need to be brave like she was.

Elizabeth Kidwell

During our life together as a general rule
You told me secrets living deep inside you
And shared them willingly because
You knew I loved you no matter what.

And generally, in wonder and sadness
As I listened, my arms held you safely
Close to my heart, and I softly smiled
Because you trusted me completely.

You never hesitated to speak the hurt
That was in your heart and mind.
I kept your secrets inner-spaced sacred
Generating in me even greater love for you.

You danced with other brave veterans
At every pow-wow, and when the drums
Ceased, I entered the Sacred Circle
To thank you for your service.

Yet, you chose not to share with me
The highest rank you achieved,
My bold and fearless general,
And I am wounded because of it.

Wounded Wings

Perhaps you failed to realize that I,
Your war widow, suffering your pain
On countless nights, had in my mind
Already granted you this superior rank.

And so my sweet general, silver star
Of my life and love, the shining truth
Is that I have been saluting you
From my deepest core all these years.

Chapter 20
Stroke

There is nothing more devastating to the human spirit than to watch the person you love most in the entire world decline in health and fade slowly away. This great sadness began for me shortly after Emi turned seventy. I was preparing breakfast in the kitchen early one morning, and Emi was setting our small kitchen table as she usually did. I turned away from the refrigerator in time to see her walk across the kitchen floor toward the dish cupboards. Without warning, she stopped suddenly and cried out, grabbing her lower back with her left hand and grasping the counter in front of her with her right to keep herself from falling. "Emi!" I shouted, instantly alarmed. "What's the matter?"

Grimacing and clearly in agony, she answered me, her voice pain loud, "Something shifted in my lower back, and it hurts to walk!" This cry was coming from the lovely woman who had shared with me not long ago that she had never suffered from a backache in her life. Alarmed that she might fall, I swung a kitchen chair behind her and helped her to sit down.

"Rest for a few minutes," I suggested, deeply concerned. As Emi rested, I finished cooking breakfast, set the table, and served up ham, eggs, and toast. Never one to miss a meal, her appetite for food often matching and fueling her appetite for life, Emi rose, as I supported her with my arm, and walked her slowly to the table. I placed an extra cushion on her chair, and she sat carefully at her customary spot in front of our kitchen picture window framing the backyard woods and ate.

After breakfast, Emi telephoned her physician's office and made an appointment for later that afternoon. X-rays revealed that arthritis had invaded Emi's spine and hips. Her doctor referred her to a pain management specialist, and after that, three or four times a year for the next seventeen years, she received cortisone injections which enabled her to live with the intense pain. I knew that her pain had to be excruciating because Emi abhorred needles and shots of any kind, but these injections she welcomed without complaint.

Each year afterwards, Emi would develop new ailments and then suffer through the resulting treatments for them. Her tenacity for living served her well. The neuropathy in her feet and legs required heavy doses of Neurontin just to keep her vertical and able to wear jeans and shoes. Eventually she also developed arthritis in her feet and nerve pain from a condition called neuroma. Her podiatrist gave her six to eight anti-inflammatory cortisone injections in each foot about every two months, and Emi endured the intense pain of these shots to get relief from greater pain, again without complaint. Her reward was always lunch at nearby Gray Brothers Cafeteria including a generous slice of their matchless apricot pie!

Later, when Emi was diagnosed with breast cancer, she bravely endured the surgery. Following her breast cancer operation, she underwent a regimen of radiation therapy and a daily dose of tamoxifen for the next ten years. The surgeon had removed the tumor from her right breast and eighteen lymph nodes from her armpit, but he made no mention of possible complications from that procedure. Emi healed happily, and bravely suffered the relentless exhaustion of radiation. By fall she was recovered enough for another adventure which took the form of an Elderhostel birding trip in North Carolina. A new school year had just begun so there was no way for me to accompany her. Surprisingly, her accommodations were in a Catholic convent, where the nuns served the participants three meals a day, buffet style. At least there, I figured, she would be safe. The nuns would look out for her. Four days into the session, Emi called me that early evening with devilment clearly on her mind and in her voice. "Ellie, I have sinned," she bragged. This was clearly not a sincere confession because Emi's voice belied contrition. She was enjoying this too much.

"What did you do to the poor nuns?" I asked, mildly amused. Emi had always relished the fact that I grew up Catholic and had spent ten years of my life in a convent. She loved to tease me about it whenever she could. So it was easy for me to picture Emi running amok in a convent, terrorizing the nuns. When I dropped her off at the airport for her flight, I had cautioned her to be kind to the sisters, who had no idea whom they would be hosting! I silently prayed that Emi had not packed her purple "Born Again Pagan" T-shirt that she was fond of wearing.

Now Emi couldn't wait to tell me. "I stole from the nuns and skipped a class!" she confessed gleefully. "Then I went bird watching and had a picnic!"

I knew that Emi would become bored with basic birdwatching classes, so I wasn't surprised. She undoubtedly could have taught the classes herself. "What did you steal from the nuns?" I asked, fearful that I would soon be receiving stolen goods.

Obviously pleased with herself, Emi confessed, "I took hard boiled eggs, bread, peanut butter, and a bottled water for my picnic!"

Relieved to learn that Emi would not be arrested, I asked, "Did you see lots of birds?"

"Oh, yes," she said laughing, as she rattled off a dozen species, "and the picnic was good, too! You would be surprised how good stolen food tastes!" Then she added, "The only bad thing was that a spider bit me on my right arm. It is a little tender and red."

By the time I picked up Emi at the airport the next evening, the arm was indeed worse, although Emi didn't tell me that until we arrived home. It is a good thing that neither of us believed in divine retribution because when Emi took off her long-sleeved shirt, I was appalled beyond words. Emi's entire right arm was swollen to twice the size of her left one! Even worse, it was red and hot to the touch.

"Emi, your arm is seriously infected!" I exclaimed. "Your welcome home party will have to wait. We are going to St. Vincent's emergency right now!" Without protest Emi climbed into my car, and twenty minutes later, an emergency room doctor examined her arm after asking all the right questions.

"The spider bite, while not poisonous, seems to have jump started two disorders which frequently follow lymph node extraction and the taking of tamoxifen," he informed us. "The first condition is lymphedema, a blockage in the lymph nodes that prevents lymph fluid in your arm from draining well, causing the swelling. The second condition that you have is cellulitis, a potentially serious skin infection which can spread to other parts of your body. We need to keep you overnight in order to give you intravenous antibiotics and to monitor your progress."

When Emi returned home the next day, the cellulitis was improved, but for the rest of her life, the lymphedema persisted. She tried wearing a compression sleeve and sleeping with her arm raised on a pillow, but the right arm from then on remained swollen with fluid. Over the years we made four more trips to the ER for cellulitis in that arm. I drove her to the hospital for three of them, but the fourth infection became so advanced overnight that Emi awoke in delirium the next morning with a temperature of 104 degrees and could not get out of bed. I had to call an ambulance. That time, she did not know who I was until late afternoon following a day of IV antibiotics. She did not remember the six emergency personnel in our house who carried her to the ambulance gurney, the trip to the hospital with the siren blaring, the six hours in the ER, or the transfer to a hospital room earlier. She had slept most of the day, and when I returned for a visit, she finally greeted me. "Hi, Bunting," she said happily, all smiles, giving me a hug.

Another time, sinus surgery at Methodist Hospital to fix her neglected broken nose and to remove a tooth embedded in her sinus cavity was the most painful. Suffering from intense pain, Emi went into a panic following the operation, believing that she could not breathe. When she awoke from the surgery, her nose was packed with gauze, and blood was draining down the back of her throat. Although the oxygen meter on her finger indicated an oxygen level of 96%, Emi struggled to breathe, constantly spitting blood out of her mouth. It broke my heart to see the pain and fear in her eyes and to hear the panic in her voice. Twice Emi pleaded into my eyes pitifully and begged, "I need oxygen!"

Promising Emi that I would see what I could do, I walked to the nurses' station to request an oxygen tube for her. "She is getting plenty of oxygen," the nurse told me when I made the request.

On my second trip to the nurses' station, I had to stand firm. "You and I know that Emi is getting adequate oxygen," I argued with the nurse politely, "but she is the patient and she doesn't feel that way. She is panicky. She will never be able to rest as long as she is anxious. Her anxiety is making her worse. The oxygen will help her psychologically."

"Who's going to pay for it?" the nurse inquired of me impatiently.

"Give her the oxygen," I insisted. "I will pay for it myself. It will be worth it to give her peace of mind." Twenty minutes later the nurse brought an oxygen tank and mask to Emi's room, and connected them. She turned on the tank, and soon as the mask was placed gently over her nose and mouth, Emi stopped struggling. Peacefully, she quieted, relaxed, and finally fell asleep with me holding her hand comfortingly. That evening the nurses offered to put a cot in Emi's room for me so that I could spend the night with her, but I had our dogs to feed and care for. Surprisingly, however, I never received a bill for the oxygen!

A few years later, Emi developed a hiatal hernia and was diagnosed with acid reflux disease and GERD. Frequently, strong stomach acid rose to burn her esophagus and throat at night. After Nexium and other medications failed to alleviate her symptoms, a doctor performed a surgical procedure called a fundoplication or "wrap," using the upper part of her stomach to wrap around her lower esophageal sphincter, creating an artificial valve and closing the hiatal hernia. Emi underwent this surgery at Community Hospital without a single complaint. The operation was a success and ended Emi's reflux problems for many years afterwards.

Eventually, even Emi's eyelids began to fail her. Thanks to gravity, large flaps of skin descended, hanging down over her eyes, blocking her vision, making driving hazardous and reading almost impossible. She had to have cosmetic surgery to correct this malady, and following the procedure, Emi's eyes never looked younger! I often teased her about having plastic surgery to look younger, and she would smile at me flirtatiously, batting her newly-young eyelids over her brown eyes. It always worked; I was hooked by those eyes!

Unfortunately, Emi's body was always sensitive to new medications, and most of the reactions occurred in the middle of the night. Though I slept upstairs, I kept my bedroom door open, and the slightest call from Emi, downstairs and three rooms away, would instantly jolt me into consciousness, usually in the wee hours of the morning. The first time this happened, I descended the stairs to find Emi lying on the dining room floor under the chandelier. She had vomited on the carpet and was writhing with stomach pain. She had just begun taking a new medication on the day before. It was three o'clock in the morning, and I was shaking from the early morning cold. I helped Emi up and walked her to a living room chair. She was miserable and cold. I covered her with an afghan, turned up the furnace temperature, and brought her clothes and shoes. After dressing her, I cleaned up the vomit, then sprinted up the stairs to get dressed myself. With my arm around her, I guided her carefully to the car and drove in the dark to St. Vincent Hospital, where we spent the next eight hours. The doctors started an IV and pumped saline and liquid Benadryl into Emi until she felt well enough to return home.

The next time Emi was trying a new medication for an infection, she climbed the stairs and touched me awake, startling me in alarm. It was 3:00 a.m. again I could see by the lighted face of the clock on my bedside table. "Emi, what's wrong?" I shouted louder than I meant to, my voice husky with sleep and instant apprehension.

The response that came from Emi was unintelligible. "Tha, tha, muh," she muttered, her eyes wide with fear that I could see even through the darkness. At that communication, I leapt out of bed and flipped on the overhead light. I stared anxiously at Emi, my heart clanging a clear warning in my chest. She tried to speak again, but I could see from her grossly-swollen tongue why she couldn't. Fearful that Emi had suffered a stroke, I knew that I had to get her to the emergency department as soon as possible. I helped her downstairs, puzzled because her movements seemed perfectly normal and there was no apparent weakness on either side. While she dressed in her bedroom, I bolted back up the stairs to do the same, and it was then that I began shaking inside and out with cold and fear. I couldn't imagine my life without Emi.

I continued trembling all the way to St. Vincent's. It wasn't until the doctors explained that Emi was having an allergic reaction to her new medication that I was able to recover from my involuntary tremors. Once again, an IV drip returned my Emi to normal as I held her hand, and her tongue gradually shrank to normal size too, so she could speak again. "Wow, that gave me a fright!" she admitted, grabbing me and holding me close. "And Darling," she continued, kissing my cheek softly, "I am so sorry that I gave you one, too!"

Unfortunately, those night trips to the hospital continued. Emi began to experience chest pains in the night, and each time she would awaken, fearing that she, like her mother before her, was suffering a heart attack. After she called me, I would routinely make her chew some orange baby aspirin. Then I would take her blood pressure, which was only slightly elevated, and follow that up by placing a tiny nitroglycerin tablet under her tongue, followed by a second one five minutes later, as her cardiologist had instructed me. I was only to drive her to the emergency ward after the third nitroglycerin failed to stop the chest pain. Then, I just dressed Emi in a robe, followed by a warm coat and moccasins for her feet and drove her to St. Vincent's emergency department to have her evaluated. Tests always confirmed that Emi had not suffered a heart attack. After a year passed and five more trips to the emergency department for chest pain, a savvy nurse happened to notice that Emi's pulse was a low 34. "That's not what it is supposed to be," she informed me. "She needs to see her cardiologist."

A subsequent visit to her heart doctor revealed that Emi's heart rate had indeed dropped over the years, slowing her down and producing her symptoms. Now at seventy-seven, it was time for Emi to get a pacemaker! Following a relatively simple surgery, and an electronically controlled consistent heartbeat of 70, Emi's energy shot up dramatically, and she never looked back as our life adventures continued. Soon, she began to wear me out once more as we continued traveling to even more beautiful places: Jekyll Island, Georgia; Point Reyes, California; Everglades, Florida; Gulf Shores, Alabama; South Padre Island, Texas; Sonoran Desert, Arizona; Nova Scotia, Canada, and Washington, D.C. Once again, I was the one struggling to keep up!

In March 2017, almost five years since Emi's death, I turned seventy, still in excellent health since my cancer surgery twenty-three years before. I wondered how this new decade would progress for me, what physical challenges I would face, and what adventures I would seek without my Emi by my side to see me through. As it turned out, I didn't have to wait long.

A month after my birthday, it felt as though an invisible finger had flipped a switch! During my yearly routine physical with my internist, she pressed on my stomach and then advised me, "When that umbilical hernia becomes painful, give me a call."

"Yes, I will," I responded. "All those years of lifting Emi off the floor have finally caught up with me, I'm afraid." More seriously, my standard blood tests revealed that I now suffered from Type II diabetes, and she referred me to an endocrinologist. The endocrinologist pulled no punches and concurred with my doctor that Metformin Extended Release tablets would be an excellent medication for me to take to control my blood sugar. What she said next took me by surprise.

"Would you remove your shoes and socks, please?" she requested firmly. Puzzled, I did as she asked, wondering what this was all about. When my feet were bare, she picked up a tuning fork and explained. "I am going to place this tuning fork against each of your toes. When you can no longer feel the vibrations, let me know." One by one, she placed the metal device against each toe, and I said "no" when I could no longer feel the tickling sensations. When she arrived at the middle toe of my right foot, strangely I felt nothing. Completing the test, the doctor laid the tuning fork down and turned to face me, delivering the bad news. "You already have diabetic peripheral neuropathy in both feet, and your middle right toe is numb."

I didn't have to ask her any questions. From my experience with Emi's neuropathy, I understood how this condition would progress: numbness, intermittent shooting pains, and eventually over the next years, intolerable foot pain requiring pain medication. I had already experienced some numbness and shooting pain in my feet and some numbness and minor pain in my hands, but so far nothing I couldn't handle. At least, I consoled myself, I would save money on shoes because of Emi. I already knew that my shoes were not the cause of my discomfort. My feet were. Welcome to the world of diabetic socks and large toe-box shoes! And eventually, like Emi, moccasins.

Two weeks later, I woke up limping from intense pain in my left foot. A visit to my neighborhood med check just six blocks away and a foot x-ray revealed the culprit. The doctor pointed to the film of my foot on the light box. A curious thing had occurred over the years. The bone spur on my left heel had made an interesting and painful 90 degree turn, and now, resembling a witch's crooked finger, it was pointing at and growing toward my toes! "You may have to have surgery on that foot," he declared. "I suggest you see an orthopedic surgeon." Oh, no, I thought to myself, foot surgery would definitely slow down my life journey. I am not ready for that yet. Besides, you show surgeons a defect, and of course they want to cut it out. It's what they do, and the pay isn't bad either! With the diabetic neuropathy already present, surgery was not my best option, I decided. I will take my chances with the pain for now. After a few days of rest and wearing my orthotics from REI, the pain subsided to tolerable, and I was back in the saddle again!

I didn't have to wait long for the next medical event. A month later I was peacefully reading a wonderful book, *Whatever...Love is Love* by actress Maria Bello, when suddenly, there was a tiny explosion of light in my left eye, followed by golden sparks and little black specks resembling dying embers in the vision of my left eye. Fearing retinal detachment, I telephoned my ophthalmologist's office and explained my symptoms. "Can you be here in an hour?" the receptionist inquired.

"Absolutely," I responded, trying to sound brave and in control.

Arriving at the office, I was quickly ushered into the doctor's examination room. Subsequent tests, examinations, and answers to questions about my peripheral vision revealed that I had suffered a posterior vitreous detachment in my left eye, not a retinal tear. "But it could develop into a retinal tear, so call my office immediately if you notice any changes in your peripheral vision or any large flashes of light in that area," the doctor warned me.

I mentally added the new terms "cobwebs, flashes, and floaters" to my vocabulary as I had all three. "I have a brown cobweb that flaps back and forth continuously from the left side of my eye to the middle and back again, while a dozen black floaters circle around," I shared with the doctor. "And at night in the dark, I see a semi-circular white flash in the left arc of my eye."

"You just have to learn to ignore these symptoms and to see though them," the doctor suggested to me. I readily agreed to do so, but the ophthalmologist was not finished with me yet. "You also have a condition called Fuchs' Dystrophy," he added, before I even had time to digest the news of the vitreous tear. "Fuchs' Dystrophy," he continued, "is a disorder where the endothelial cells that protect the cells of the corneas of both eyes die off slowly. The corneas lose that protection, and fluid begins to build up within each cornea, causing thickening, eventual blurring, and possibly blindness. Here is a pamphlet that explains the disorder."

"Wow!" I exclaimed, staring at the pamphlet in my hands and feeling a bit overwhelmed with this added bad news. "Is there any good news about my eyes today?"

"Yes!" the doctor responded enthusiastically, obviously trying to cheer me up. "There are no signs of diabetic retinopathy at this visit; your cataracts are still small, and you have 20/20 vision with your glasses! Just keep on taking your eye vitamins so you don't develop macular degeneration."

At his words I smiled and stifled my impulse to laugh. I remembered the positive news that Emi and I had always looked for in every negative situation. We consistently found reasons to smile and laugh. Life for us might often have taken us one step back, but our love for each other and our pure joy in living, always moved us two steps forward in response. In that way we constantly stayed ahead of unhappiness. Humor and love bound us together, and in my mind I could still hear her happy voice reminding me, "That's two things wrong, but *three* things right!"

Fortified with so many life-affirming memories, I am not afraid to face the next ten or more years of my life alone, however long I have left. I am deeply blessed to have lived for twenty-five years with the best example of positive living I could ever have dreamed of: a woman who relished every moment of life with me and never wasted it. Emi always turned negative news into positive challenges. She was the "bravest of the brave," and now to honor her memory, I am determined to live bravely and to spend the rest of my life discovering and celebrating its joys.

Wounded Wings

It was a stroke of luck
When I first met you,
Gazed deeply into your lively, brown eyes,
Recognized a new, forever friend
And loved you.

Naturally, it was a stroke of genius
Which allowed me to understand
That not only would you become my best friend,
But you would be so much more:
My exceptional lover,
My excellent partner,
The love of my life.

Soon, with just the stroke of a pen
We made life legal:
We would share everything
Together, equally
And become a close, loving family
Under one roof.

Happily, with a stroke of brilliance,
You gave me a second childhood,
Showed me astounding beauty,
And encouraged me to wonder at the world,
Which you dropped softly
into my waiting hands.

Elizabeth Kidwell

Eventually, with a stroke of light,
I realized how bright, meaningful, and rich
My poor life had become
In your blessed presence,
As you gifted me every moment
With your love.

Then, with a stroke of insight,
I finally understood that everything
I ever wanted was standing right before me,
Grinning back with wild merriment
And quiet humor,
Hands outstretched to hold me
Every minute if I would let you.

Sadly, at the stroke of midnight,
A silent killer struck you down,
Robbed you of movement and freedom,
But never of the will to live.
As ever your warm, sweet hand held mine,
And your brown and lively eyes
Danced love all around me
Until you closed them for the last time.

Chapter 21
Inflight

The strongest bond which Emi and I shared was our love of nature and birds. Though we were almost twenty-three years apart in age, both of us had lived childhoods that were primarily spent outdoors. We cherished personal freedom, beautiful spaces, intriguing nature, and especially the mystery of birds.

Emi spent her childhood summers at Turkey Run State Park in Indiana, and her young adulthood bicycling across the New England States and across Europe. Her thirties, forties, and fifties were spent with Beth, traveling and bird watching across the globe in exotic places like Kenya, Hawaii, Costa Rica, England, Scotland, and the Galapagos.

In contrast, my childhood was spent in the San Joaquin River Valley of central California not too far from Benicia Bay and the San Joaquin River delta where bird life was abundant especially during the winter months. I lived my young adulthood in Los Angeles and the foothills of the California Coastal Range with visits to my parents' small ranch on the San Joaquin River delta, and an occasional visit to the Grizzly Island Wildlife Preserve between Suisun Bay and Grizzly Bay. At these places I enjoyed the wonders of birds like burrowing owls, cinnamon teal, loggerhead shrikes, tri-colored blackbirds, western sandpipers, dunlins, willets, pheasant, white-tailed kites, American avocets, California towhees, and golden eagles, just to name a few.

It only took a short time after Emi and I met and discovered our common interests that we became fast friends. Over the next six months, with a love of exploration, adventure, and discovery already in our blood, we bonded as one without question and never looked back.

One of our first birding trips together occurred in early November 1988, as we drove to the Jasper-Pulaski Fish and Wildlife Area in northern Indiana. Once there, we marveled at some of the 10,000 migrating sandhill cranes using the lowland swampy areas of the preserve as a stop-over. People always heard them before they saw them, loudly squawking as they soared high in the sky in V formation, perhaps encouraging all members of their family groups to fly on. Once they landed awkwardly, these large birds bowed and leaped like ballet dancers, greeting each other in a flurry of feathers. They performed the dance over and over again. It was a sight I will never forget! Emi and I stood on the high wooden viewing platform with our binoculars and spotting scope, mesmerized for hours by their glorious choreography and performance.

Another early trip during our first summer together was to the New England States. While we enjoyed birdwatching along Cape Cod, the New Jersey shoreline, and the coasts of Connecticut and Rhode Island, Maine was our favorite state. A visit to breathtaking Acadia National Park on Mount Desert Island, coastal cool even in mid-summer, revealed empty eider nests on the shore of Bar Harbor. The nests were lined with down pulled from the selfless common eiders' own bodies, and this sacrifice had kept their eggs and nestlings warm. Not too far offshore, small rafts of common eiders were dotted here and there with a few beautiful and impressive king eiders, two lifer birds for me!

Sometimes on our nature journeys, we never even saw the birds we counted! A road trip to visit friends in St. Louis, Missouri, culminated in an evening drive to some country woods outside of the city. There we delighted in the onomatopoeic calls of the nightjars, secretive birds that fly at night, catching insects on the wing. The two nightjars we heard this night were the small whippoorwills and the larger chuck will's-widows. In the dark the birds alternated their calls, jarring the silence of the night to identify themselves. The insistent call of "whip-poor-will, whip-poor-will, whip-poor will," was chorused by slightly louder calls, "Chuck-will's widow, Chuck-will's widow, Chuck-will's widow!" After an hour of fascinated listening and two more lifer birds for me, we tired and drove back to our friends' house in the city, but the secretive, night-loving birds, we knew, would keep up their self-identifying chorus all night long, preferring to sleep during the day.

Another secretive bird is the American woodcock, so elusive to me that by millennium 2000, I had still not seen one, but that was about to change. One fine April morning, Emi was busy, so I took our dog Tyler, a small white shepherd mix, for company and drove south along

Interstate 65 to Camp Atterbury Fish and Wildlife Preserve, forty miles away. I parked my car near a meadow, and with Tyler on lead, hiked across the open field toward a small distant stand of trees. With my dog slightly ahead of me, we arrived at the edge of the small woods, when suddenly, Tyler spooked in alarm, rearing backwards against me as a brown blur whirled straight up in front of him, wings emitting a twittering sound as it flew high into the trees and out of sight. Shaken by the experience, Tyler and I changed directions, which as it turned out, was the best decision I could have made.

When I arrived home that afternoon, I shared my experience with Emi. She was instantly curious and amused. "Next Saturday, we are going to Camp Atterbury," she announced, a knowing smile on her face. True to her word, the following Saturday morning we packed a lunch and headed south in Emi's old VW Golf. We parked in the same spot and hiked toward the woods this time without a dog. Along the way, Emi spoke softly, "Try to remember where you encountered the bird, but walk very slowly and carefully." I nodded silently and took Emi's hand as we crept toward the area. Emi had already prepared me that if the bird was a woodcock, she would have a camouflaged nest on the ground. We approached the spot in complete silence. Suddenly, just as before, the brown bird at our feet shot skyward in alarm. "Stop! Don't move!" Emi commanded, and I froze instantly. Emi stared down at the ground in front of us. "Look here," she said pointing to a simple depression covered in leaves at our feet. Four medium-sized, tan-brown mottled eggs stared up at us. "There is the nest!" While I watched, Emi pulled out of her pocket the clean, white, cotton handkerchief that she habitually carried, unfolded it, and tied it securely to the branch of a small bush growing directly above the nest. "Now we go away for a while," she announced. "I think that this would be an excellent time to eat lunch!"

We ate our sandwiches and fruit while perched on a low-hanging branch of a tree along peaceful Sugar Creek, and then hiked back to the tiny woods. Even from a distance Emi's handkerchief signaled to us. We slowed as we approached, and Emi reached out her hand to stop me silently as we neared the nest. Looking down in the location of the nest, we spied the female woodcock sitting on it at our feet. As long as we moved no closer, she would stay there, giving us plenty of time to admire her. This bird was large and chunky with a long, tapered bill, well-camouflaged by mottled feathers of light and dark brown. If she was nervous, she didn't show it, but kept her post, eyes wide open, fearlessly protecting her eggs. For some time we gazed in wonder at my new "lifer" bird. Then Emi reached up, untied her handkerchief, and we silently backed away. On our walk back to the car, Emi was pleased with herself and me. "Got yourself a lifer today, didn't cha?" she bragged, grinning widely.

"Yes, thanks to you!" I exclaimed, enfolding her in my arms in a great big hug.

As it turned out, I only had to wait until the end of the following March to see a male woodcock. Eagle Creek Park in Indianapolis held an annual birding event each spring just at sundown in a specific area of the park where a meadow met the woods. It was spring cold, so avid bird watchers, including Emi and me, arrived still bundled in winter jackets and huddled together for warmth, anticipating a wondrous show. We didn't have long to wait. Almost on cue, a male woodcock began "peenting" on the ground in the dusky twilight. "Peent! Peent! Peent!" he sang insistently to a nearby female. Suddenly, he shot straight up into the air, whistling and performing his sky dance, all the while "peenting." Then, he plummeted to the ground, landing next to the chosen female that he was trying to impress and making kissing sounds before taking to the sky once again. I stood, too mesmerized by the show to feel cold. Beside me, Emi was smiling happily, squeezing my gloved hand three times.

Of course, as far as we were concerned, no birding experience would be more complete than a trip along the Sonoma California coast to Bodega Bay, where Alfred Hitchcock had filmed his classic thriller, *The Birds*! Near there, we went out of our way somewhat to gather a new fort for Emi. The Russian-built Fort Ross had been the base of the Russian fur trade in California, an operation, which had practically decimated the sea otter and fur seals in the area, but thankfully spared the bird populations.

After spending a restful night at the Bodega Bay Lodge, Emi and I rose at dawn, the best time to view birds, whose main concern at this early hour was catching breakfast. We bundled up against the early morning foggy mist and grabbed our binoculars. After a short drive to Bodega Harbor, we parked the car and walked briskly toward the shallow, rocky inlet, a natural bird magnet and one of America's best birding spots. On the shore before us, black turnstones, ruddy turnstones, and spotted sandpipers bobbed along the low tide mud flats, flipping shells and pebbles in their search for food. Out in the deep, calm water, Western grebes, Clark's grebes, and surf scoters rose and fell on the undulating waves, occasionally diving for small fish. Beyond the bay both white and brown pelicans skimmed the surf in small groups, also seeking fish. This was a birder's paradise for sure, and today my Emi, with almost 700 bird species on her North American life list, was about to come face to face with a new lifer bird!

We picked our way along the rocky shore and returned to the safer boardwalk of the harbor. Walking was easier here, and it offered a higher vantage point from which to view birds in the harbor. Our eyes swept over the large raft of sea birds that rode low in the surf farther out, but with our binoculars we easily identified them as Pacific loons, with their soft grey heads and black throats, lifers for me, of course! When we lowered our binoculars, there he was, bobbing rhythmically on the water right in front of us only five yards out, staring at up us, curiously unafraid. He lifted his head so that even with our naked eyes, we could easily admire his striking brick-red throat, his outstanding bird identification feature. "Hot damn!" Emi exclaimed softly beside me so as not to frighten this beautiful bird. She didn't even have to consult her bird identification guide. "It's a red-throated loon, a lifer for me!"

"And for me," I said, delighted to share our discovery. It was a simple task to mark the date and place where we saw this species in our old National Geographic field guides. The red-throated loon was the first bird pictured in our guides to North American birds! Emi grabbed me and we hugged fiercely in joy, dancing up and down.

"We finally got the first bird!" my beloved woman chirped happily.

It was during that first Christmas in California after I lost Emi when I discovered that I no longer enjoyed bird watching. For no apparent reason, I had packed Emi's smaller, better Leitz binoculars, although I had no intention of using them. Two weeks after I arrived, when my niece and nephew had returned to school, Louise and Eugene drove me to beautiful Point Pinole Regional Park near San Pablo, where wintering birds were abundant. They hoped to give me an enjoyable experience that would ease my pain and make my sadness a little more bearable. They were so sweet, loving, and kind that I didn't have the heart to tell them how much this park visit was hurting me. I let them walk ahead of me, while I lagged behind, pretending interest in the water birds near the pier. I would lift Emi's binoculars to my eyes periodically, but I saw nothing because tears clouded my vision. I was relieved that day when it was time to return to Oakland and pick up the kids.

Little by little, despite my failure to see anything through Emi's binoculars, I began to realize why I had brought them along. Of all Emi's many possessions, and there were hundreds, this was the one that had always brought wonder and beauty up close for her. The "binocs," as we called them, had accompanied her on every outdoor trip of her adult life even before I knew her, and they had always seemed a part of her, secured to her body by a shoulder harness, keeping her hands free, but always ready to grab when she needed to view wonders up close. While she primarily used the binoculars for bird identification, she learned countless lessons by looking through the lenses. She studied animals, insects, trees, flowers, mountains, rivers, waterfalls, oceans, fish, whales, and even people through those eyepieces. With them, she gathered the world up close, delighted and amazed by nature's secrets. But I always believed in my heart that she was seeing so much more, realities she could not describe to me. By using her binoculars, I sought to improve my vision, to understand the world positively as she had, and to bring the realities of life in closer so that I could once again feel a part of living instead of the distant alienation I now felt. Since Emi's devastating loss, I had lived disconnected, aloof, alone, lost, shrinking into myself a little more each day. I didn't know if I could recover from her death, and saddest of all, I wasn't sure that I wanted to. So gradually, imperceptibly each day, I continued to fold up, believing in my heart and mind, that I was the only one suffering, and no one could really understand the depth of my loss. So for the most part, my bird-watching days ended when Emi died. I was too busy trying to cope with the massive hole in my heart, with the pain that would not quit, no matter what I did day or night. The only birds I paid attention to were the ones in the backyard, birds I believed in my heart that Emi had sent with little messages, as she had once promised, and those silent missives usually chirped to my mind, "Have courage."

Courage is not what I felt. I felt ruined inside with the devastation that nothingness brings. I had dreaded the thought of her possible loss throughout our partnership, while praying for mine first, but I had never dwelled on it because we were too busy living and loving. Now that Emi was gone, I did nothing but dwell on it. I was earthbound and grief bound. My loss of her was my sole reality. Zombie-like, I went through the motions of each day, speaking from my hollowness with friends and family, who loved me enough to support me, though I often remembered nothing that they said. I don't know how they viewed me during that first year, but to me, their love and support felt like pain because it was not Emi's. Where had I gone? What had happened to me? All I knew was that I was not with Emi, and that was the only place I wanted to be, the only place where I could possibly feel happy again. She had been the light of my world, and now that light was gone. I was stumbling around each day in the darkness of my own clouded mind, and I wanted it to end.

Eventually, I had discovered that mindfulness walking and breathing helped calm my anxieties, so each day I tried to take a long walk along the Central Canal, which formed the northern boundary of our Butler-Tarkington neighborhood. To get to the canal trail, I had to walk along Westfield Boulevard for a short distance before crossing the blue bridge to the safer side of the canal. One morning, I was walking along busy Westfield, cars and trucks whizzing past me. I could feel the power of speeding steel as each vehicle blew by me with incredible force. Suddenly I looked up and saw a large, white pickup truck approaching me at high speed in the nearest lane. *Just step out in front of it,* I told myself. *The pain will end.* And just as swiftly, another stronger, kinder voice in my mind answered, dragging me forcibly back into the real world, *Yes, and what about the driver who will unintentionally kill you? What about his life? How will he live with this forever?* The loud voice blotted out any other thought. *You have no right to put him through that.* The side draft made by the truck as it rumbled past me pushed me back from the street. In a few short seconds, I had opened the door to reality and stepped through, making my first conscious decision to live.

Returning home, the first thing I did was to call Ellen, my grief therapist. When she answered, I said simply, "I think that I need to see you very soon."

"I have an opening at 11:00 a.m. tomorrow. Would that work for you?" she replied.

"Oh, yes!" I said. "Thank you."

The next morning I sat across from Ellen in my usual comfortable spot and sadly shared with her the event of the day before, when I had felt so desperate to end my pain. She listened attentively and knowingly, not showing any surprise in the least. "What I don't understand," I said finally, "was that insistent voice in my head stopping me."

Ellen didn't hesitate in the least. "That," she explained smiling, "was a perfect example of real compassion. You put a complete stranger ahead of you and your pain. You did not want him to suffer any emotional or physical pain because you know what that feels like." Then she added, "I believe that you have made a positive breakthrough in your grief journey."

Elizabeth Kidwell

I now go birdwatching alone
Using your binoculars,
Hoping to improve my vision,
Looking through your eyes
At the wonder all around me,
Viewing from a closer distance,
A deeper penetration
Into birds, into life.
I cry now always
When I walk the paths
We use to walk together
Or even a new one
We never shared.

I see birds through tears now,
Dissolving them
Into puddles of color
That drip from my eyes,
Down my face until
I no longer recognize
The flight in them.
Regardless of who accompanies
Me on these watchful journeys,
I am alone in my thoughts,
My point of view pointless
Until I think of how excited
You became even when you viewed
The same bird for the hundredth time,
For you, never a loss for
The initial awe of feathers and flight.

Wounded Wings

I need your insight, inflight really,
To correct my vision inward
As well as outward.
I need to observe more than birds,
To see clearly
How to fly freely in my mind
With soft wings.

This journey of discovery, my love,
I must walk and fly without you.
For the present I am grounded:
Wounded wings,

No clear flight plan for the future,
No takeoff for freedom yet,
Far from soaring toward the sunbird
Of healing warmth and penetrating light
In the downdraft of utter compassion.

Chapter 22
Natural Process

During our twenty-five years together, Emi only worried about one thing: what would happen to me after she died, leaving me to face this world on my own. She understood only too well how fragile I was. She also knew how devastated I would be when she left me because she had suffered the loss of her beloved Beth. Even more important, she had learned through our partnership that it was possible to love and to laugh deeply again after losing that one person who mattered most in all the world. Once she met me, it had taken Emi almost a year to love me deeply. While somewhat distressing for me at the time, I believed it happened because in her mind, she was comparing me to Beth, and I often fell short. I, on the other hand, had fallen in love with Emi right from the start, even before I knew every secret fact about her. I just felt that she was the one who spoke to my spirit and delighted my heart from the very beginning, even during our first six months of friendship, and I trusted her completely. I know now that Emi could have provided me with so many insights into loss and grief had I let her share them with me from her own personal experience, but losing her to death was a topic I never wanted to discuss, and I found the prospect of Beth's loss too sad to talk about then, although Emi wanted to. By the time I needed to talk to her about her grief journey, it was too late.

Because Emi had found love a second time with me, she embarked on a campaign that she thought would make it possible for me to find love again in the event of her death. We had been together happily for five years when Emi first began her efforts. Part of her urgency lay in the fact that because both her parents had died at a relatively young age, she believed in the possibility that she would too. She also knew that it had taken her five years to find me after Beth died, and given my age, she did not want me to wait that long to find companionship. The fact was, however, that Emi had never stopped mourning her beloved Beth. In reality, her grief had become part of our relationship, too. From the countless stories Emi had told me about their travels and escapades,

I felt Beth's strong presence in our lives. Her photographs, as well as mine, adorned Emi's bedroom walls. I was even introduced to Beth's three children when we traveled to St. Louis, Missouri. Besides that, Beth's daughter, two granddaughters, and her only great-granddaughter often stayed with us several times a year. If I had passed Beth on the street, I would have recognized her, no stranger to me! Yet never once did I ever believe that I had taken Beth's place. That was impossible! I was just another woman whom Emi grew to love with all her heart, never a replacement. I realized in delight over the years that Emi had so much love to give that she had filled two women's lives with joy and laughter, fifty-five years' worth in total! Her life was that powerful.

I was so totally in love with Emi that the fear of losing her was a palpable presence within me. For the most part, I chose to ignore that specter, to be happy in my life with her, and not to worry about the future. Despite my efforts to focus on quality living, every single one of Emi's medical conditions or accidental physical injuries over the years brought up that old anxiety again, and I battled within myself against that fear because I knew how very tenuous life was, and how in just one second, everything could change.

So it was that Emi began her campaign to secure a promise from me following just about every health crisis she suffered. It all started when Emi reached her sixty-eighth birthday. I recognized right away that her concern stemmed from her mother's death and Beth's death, both at the age of sixty-nine. Doing all that was humanly possible to keep Emi healthy and happy, I was caught off-guard by Emi's request. "Darling," she began one afternoon, "you know that someday I will die…." She never finished her sentence. Immediately, I burst into tears and had to be held and comforted. Whatever else she as going to say that day was never verbalized.

A year later Emi tried to bring up the subject again. "Bunting," she said to me one lovely day, catching me completely off guard, "when I die, I don't want you to be alone." My response was the same: I wailed as if she had just broken my heart.

Through my tears I managed to sob, "You are not going to die! I won't have it!" The discussion that Emi hoped to have stopped right then.

Yet, Emi was persistent. Every year after that, possibly when she thought I was in a positive space, she would bring the subject up again, despite the fact that for the most part, she was in good health.

"Darling," she began gently one morning while we were still sitting in the kitchen after breakfast, "as difficult as it is for you, we must discuss the future when I am no longer here." She took my hands in her own and gazed lovingly but seriously into my eyes, which had already begun to fill with tears. I couldn't understand what else she wanted since we had already made out our wills and our durable powers of attorney. I thought that the business of losing her was already covered. I could never have been more wrong. I gazed sadly into her sweet, brown eyes, and she loved me back with hers. "When I die," she continued, "I want you to find someone else to love."

There they were finally, the words I never wanted to hear. No wailing this time, but my tears flowed faster as I answered her, my words choked by anguish, "My Love, don't you understand that there will be no one after you? You are the love of my life. And when it is time for you to die, I will let you know. Until then, let's just enjoy our life together not worry about it." Again the topic was dropped for another year.

Somewhat frustrated with me, Emi began her own preparations for death. Perhaps she understood how useless I would be when she left this life, so she decided to have everything ready. First, she wrote her own obituary. She left specific instructions for the type of memorial service she wanted. She also changed mortuaries and prepaid her cremation. She even left specific instructions for me as to where to place her cremains. Sheet after sheet of preparations were printed out and bound into a red notebook. On the cover she clearly printed the words, "In the event of my death." She placed them carefully with other red folders in her wooden file and showed me where to find them. Then at my suggestion, she began to use her drawer full of family pictures to create albums, highlighting different periods of her life and the people she loved. She ended up with a dozen binders. "These are to be displayed at my memorial service," she instructed while I was reading them. Intrigued by details of her life I never knew, I promised her I would.

Following her year of preparation, my hope had been that his would signal the end of Emi's campaign, but I was so wrong. Emi was the most dearly stubborn person I knew, and once again she kept up her yearly request. "Darling, promise me that you will find someone to love after I die. I don't want you to be alone. See how well it worked out for me after Beth died?"

My answer was always the same, "There can be no one else."

So the next time Emi brought up the topic, I had heard enough. To put an end to this subject for once and for all, I promised her that I would find someone else, but in my heart I knew it was a lie, the only lie I had ever told her. Emi seemed content finally, and she never brought up the topic again. She believed that I would be true to my word, and she was at peace.

During the year after I lost Emi, however, I was never at peace. My grief made that impossible. Inexplicably though, seven months after Emi died, I began to focus obsessively on that one lie that I had told her. I had always kept my promises to her, and in my sad, lonely mind, I felt her exacting this promise from me. I had to do something about it, although I was not ready for a new relationship in the least. Despite the fact that Ellen, my grief therapist, had warned me against making any important decisions or changes in my life during the first year following a loss, my promise to Emi trumped her cautionary advice. While I was visiting my sister and her family in California that first winter without Emi, I began to focus only on that promise, fueled by a persistent, palpable, heartbreaking loneliness.

The one advantage I had over Emi's search thirty years before was the Internet. I discovered dozens of meet-up sites on the Web. Self-centered in my own grief, I never considered the millions of lonely people in the world. The Internet quickly revealed to me the extent of this global sadness. To my surprise, however, I quickly found a meet-up site called L-Date. I paid for a three-month membership, and magically within one day, I was communicating with a lovely-sounding woman from snowy Vermont! She said that she was only a few months younger than me and had Native American ancestry through the Blackfeet tribe. I was delighted to exchange emails through the site, and every time she responded, I felt a little less lonely. Two months later I shared with her that I was a recent widow. What I discovered at the end of three months was that she was married, but her wife was in a care facility suffering from Alzheimer's disease. I recognized then that there were losses greater than mine. Although I invited her to continue corresponding with me through my regular email or by telephone, she declined. The distance between us and the fact that she was married lessened the disappointment and hurt I felt from her rejection despite the fact that I had never heard her voice. Technically, I had already fulfilled the promise I had made to Emi. I had tried to find someone. That should have been enough.

Because of my incredible loneliness, however, it wasn't enough. A few weeks later, my friend Lee was visiting, and I asked him how long he had waited following the death of his wife to cancer, before he started his search for his lovely new wife Kat. "Four months," he answered.

"And where did you meet her?" I inquired, thinking that they may have met at a cancer survivor support group since Kat's husband had also died of cancer.

"We met on match.com," he said. I mistakenly believed that match.com was a meet-up service exclusively for heterosexuals, but Lee set me straight. "Oh, no," he informed me, "you can meet anyone on match.com. They even have sections for women to meet women and for men to meet men!" Heartened by this information, I decided to try it, despite gentle warnings from Ellen. I had no idea of the coming troubles that would only add more pain to my heavy, burdensome grief. I was desperate to feel some relief, so once again, I tried to take a shortcut.

I contacted match.com online and paid for a six-month membership. Then I began searching. As soon as I completed my profile and submitted it without a photo, I began to receive dozens of responses from women of every age and nationality from everywhere in the United States and Canada! I was amazed at first and a little flattered that women in their twenties, thirties, and forties could be interested in a sixty-five-year-old woman. Foolishly, I actually responded by site email to a very young blonde from California, informing her that I was too old for her! The sheer number of strangers trying to contact me should have alarmed me, but once again, I was eager to end my pain, and my heart paid no attention to the feeble warning light that went off in my mind. I read through every profile of the women who had reached out to me through the website, but only settled on two women because they lived in Indiana and sounded kind.

The first woman I emailed was Hannah. I was searching for someone closer to my own age, but she was six years older. After a short discussion with Ellen about age, I thought, close enough. I would give her a try even though she lived in northern Indiana, about three hours away. I contacted her through match.com, and she responded immediately. We exchanged letters for a few days on the site. Then Hannah gave me her personal email address and invited me to write to her directly. After a few more days, she gave me her home phone number and invited me to call. Hannah had recently lost her life-partner, a psychologist, to cancer. She told me that she had been a therapist also, but that fact never seemed to help her during her own grief journey. She had to seek out a lesbian grief therapist, as I had. I learned that Hannah now spent her time creating and firing unique pottery figures and selling them online. She appeared to be educated and creative at seventy-two, so I took a chance and called her.

Hannah answered on the fourth ring. When she said hello, I found her voice to be deep and friendly. I introduced myself, and she didn't seem surprised. We had shared so much in our emails that we needed little further introduction. Our conversation seemed easy and uncomplicated, as Hannah began to reveal stories of the relationship she had shared with the love of her life. I listened deeply and thoughtfully. "Early in our relationship," Hannah told me, "my partner always maintained that she was not a lesbian. One day I asked her why she would think that. Her answer was that lesbians loved women, but she just loved me!" At Hannah's words, we both shared deep, life-affirming laughter, which signaled to me that we would both be all right. My laughter surprised me because since Emi's death, nothing was funny, and I never expected to experience the joy of laughter ever again. I felt grateful toward Hannah for showing me that I could. Joy could become part of my life again, I realized.

Then I asked her, "Hannah, when did you know that your grief period was over?"

Kindly, she answered, "When I stopped crying."

"How long did that take?" I asked curiously, since I was still crying every single day.

"A year and a half for me," she shared generously, "but it varies with each person." After more than two hours of conversation, we hung up. That evening I composed a poem about friendship and laughter and emailed it to her as a way of saying thanks. The next day, we spoke again, and after thanking me for the poem, Hannah requested that I email her a photograph of myself. I agreed and carefully chose a photo taken at a cousin's recent wedding that showed me dressed up and almost smiling. I knew my photo would not compare to the lovely and intelligent Rachel Maddow from CNN, whom Hannah admired and often spoke about, and whose television program she admitted watching each night, but I sent it anyway.

That was the last time that I ever heard from Hannah. Inexplicably, she never returned any of my emails or telephone calls again. Ellen, who had been delighted to hear that I was communicating with a retired therapist, seemed confused and disappointed at the news. She worked to help me get past this latest rejection that only compounded my grief. Many months later, Hannah, perhaps having second thoughts, attempted to friend me on Facebook, but sadly, by that time, I no longer trusted her with my feelings and had moved on.

What I had moved on to was a nightmare of my own making, and I was not prepared for the intensity of the passion, pain, and confusion I was to suffer. Worst of all, in my own grief-crazed mind, I believed that Emi had sent this woman to me. Why I felt this way would not be clear to me for a long time. The woman's name was Christa, and she lived in Indianapolis, just sixteen miles away. On the outside she was a dark, attractive older woman with black eyes and black and silver hair. She was half Cherokee, slim and lovely, slightly taller than me. She had a smile that lit up the room and my heart warmed to her immediately. When I first met her, she seemed shy and nervous, not sure of herself. I could never have been more wrong. She knew exactly what she was doing because she had thirty years of practice before I came along.

When she first contacted me through match.com, she lied and said that she was sixty-five. It wasn't until I was already smitten by her charms that she admitted she was seventy.

That first lie should have been enough warning, especially after a friend pointed out, "It makes you wonder what else she is lying about," but I made excuses for it since she looked younger. Not realizing how very weak I was, I allowed myself during the months that followed to be sucked into a cruel game of pull me close, then push me away, as a form of manipulation. There would be three weeks of close togetherness, sweet beyond belief, a dream come true, followed by two weeks of rejection and no contact. In addition, I was being played off against another woman she had also met on match.com and lived in Indianapolis, who was probably suffering similar confusion. I felt as if my head was being twisted off like a cap off a bottle, and that Christa wanted total control of my life. Intimacy with her, though sweet at first, became a bargaining chip for getting what she wanted. The pain and confusion I felt was doubled by the grief I was still suffering over the loss of Emi. I felt like I was drowning all over again. Ellen tried to help during my therapy sessions as once again I cried through pain and loss. The progress I had made during the past six months began to disintegrate before the onslaught of Christa's heartless game playing and her attempts to isolate me from my friends and family. I had never experienced anything like this in my life. As each of her cycles repeated, my original passion for Christa slowly dwindled and deteriorated, but the aftermath of my terrible mistake lay in the horrendous destruction of my feelings of self-worth and self-confidence. I felt beaten-down and defeated every single day by her verbal abuse and demands, while still striving to regain my mental footing and self-respect. Saddest of all, I learned that Christa had successfully preyed upon other lesbians who had also suffered the loss of their long-time partners. Her aim was to enrich herself with what they owned, and in their weakness, they willingly gave all to her just to be with her. I was no different. In my weakness and infatuation for her, I loaned her a large sum of money, which was never repaid. I had been taken advantage of and duped. I was so ashamed of myself.

So, to cope with and to survive my double sadness, I had to face inward to rediscover the inner strength and courage I knew I possessed, my strong core that had seen me through so many of the disappointments and trials of life. In my weakness I had been looking to others for these gifts, when all the while, they already existed within me. Believe me when I say that there is no shortcut to grief. It is a natural process which takes years to complete. When there is a hole in your heart, it is natural to want to plug up that hole with someone to stop the pain and the bleeding. But that tendency, I learned through experience, is a grave mistake. Emotional bleeding is a way to cleanse inner wounds, carrying away what festers in the heart, until purified, it is able to heal on its own. Where once I couldn't stand to be alone, I gradually began to delight in my healing solitude, and I realized that I was right all along. No one can ever take Emi's place. I was blessed beyond measure with twenty-five years of her earthly love, and now I enjoy an eternity of her spirit love. I don't have to look any further than my own self-love for comfort. I am truly content being the person I am finally without Emi's physical presence. I kept my promise to Emi, and I have grown wiser through this experience, though as I was to learn, Emi wasn't finished with my lessons yet.

Nothing about grief seems natural to me.
Naturally, I miss you more than my life,
But not more than life itself. You saw to that.

You knew it was not in my nature to be strong
When faced with so much sorrow and this
Incredible loss, so you taught me courage
Just for this time, which we knew would someday come,
Yet still so unexpected.

Naturally, tears free-flow down my face
Daily, a liquid mess, and I allow them to go,
Watering the parched earth of my mind to keep thought alive.
Naturally, my first waking thought each morning
Turns to you, and my last memory at night
Is illuminated with the only person I meet in my dreams.

Since missing you is a natural process, there will be
No drug, no drink, no magic potion to deaden pain.
Grief will be taken head on, face to the wind,
Without respite, without warning, without sleep.

Naturally, I am not myself anymore; a pale reflection
Has replaced the person, who with frequent smiles
And happy laughter once charged into the uncertain world
Because then, naturally, I had your love to hold me.

So, where am I going without your life-love is a natural question
For which I have no answer. It is so lonely making this journey
Without you, but I keep on searching to see where it leads…
Naturally.

Chapter 23
Midnight Sun

June 1996 was a memorable time for Emi and me. We were in the middle of our trip to Alaska, and we had arrived in Fairbanks by bus from Denali National Park and Preserve, where we had viewed all 20,000 snow-covered feet of "The Great One" in glittering sunlight, just in time for the Festival of the Midnight Sun. Because of its close proximity to the Arctic Circle, Fairbanks was blessed with twenty-four hours of daylight during the summer. On the twenty-first of June, summer solstice, the sun never dips below the horizon, so it was possible to enjoy the beautiful sight of the Midnight Sun, low in the sky.

Because of so much light and endless day, activities were continuous, and numerous festivals celebrated this light-filled phenomenon. The Fairbankans stay awake for twenty-four hours to participate or spectate in the Midnight Soccer Tourney, the Midnight Sun Baseball Game, the Midnight Sun Fun Run, the Yukon 800 Riverboat Race, the Midnight Sun Dance, the Chantanika Music Festival, and shopping under the Midnight Sun. There were also special trips available to view the Midnight Sun from local mountaintops. Emi and I were amazed at how much outdoor fun Fairbankans crammed into the summer months, so as not to waste any precious sunlight. We too reveled in the fact that we could play for twenty-four hours and never lose sunlight. These truly were our kind of people, and although we tried to keep up with them, we found ourselves dropping into bed at 2:00 a.m., while outside our windows, which featured blackout curtains, the townspeople continued to revel in their hikes, baseball games, and picnics!

During our second day in Fairbanks, we booked a four-hour riverboat tour on the *Discovery*, an authentic Alaskan sternwheeler, to explore the sites along the Chena River. The cruise included watching bush pilots taking off and landing on the river and an hour tour of Chena Indian Village, where we learned about the Athabaskan fur trade, salmon smoking and preserving, and their artistic creations of beautiful beadwork. The *Discovery* also took us to an incredible place called "the wedding of the waters," where the Chena and Tanana Rivers joined. Here, the cloudy, glacial waters of the Tanana met the clear Chena waters in a spectacular display!

Emi's favorite part of the *Discovery* cruise was a stop at the summer home of famous musher, Susan Butcher. By 1996, Susan had already won the Iditarod sled dog race four times. She was only the second woman to win the grueling race. Both Emi and I admired her for the strength and courage she showed in her pursuit of excellence and in her love of dogs. The sternwheeler pulled up alongside the shore at Susan's summer compound including a cabin and dog kennels, where she and her husband David Monson trained their dogs using wheels on the sleds instead of snow runners. Unfortunately, that day Susan was busy in the cabin caring for the couple's first baby, so David, also a musher, was the one who demonstrated their sled dog training and introduced us to their famous dogs.

When the paddle wheeler returned to the home dock, Emi and I disembarked to visit the gift shop. At the entrance stood a life-sized cardboard display of Susan Butcher standing behind her famous sled. Emi stepped into the scene, and I snapped her photo! Then, Emi discovered an appropriate T-shirt that read, "Alaska: where men are men, and women win the Iditarod again, and again and again." Needless to say, she bought it as a souvenir, and for years afterwards, she wore that shirt at least once a week! She loved it!

Our next excursion in Fairbanks was a fan boat trip down one of the many shallow river tributaries, which terminated near a gold-dredging camp. Forget the panning for gold! The real thrill of the trip was the invigorating nonstop skimming down a river with only six inches of water in it! The huge whirling fan at the back of the boat propelled us forward at breakneck speeds! Exhilarated by the velocity we reached skimming the top of the shallows while the pilot deftly swerved right then left to avoid large stones in our way, Emi and I laughed at the danger like the daredevils we were! The experience was totally bracing and snappy! The zooming ride back to port was equally thrilling. We loved it! Best of all, the daylight in which to experience and to enjoy it all was endless!

Years later, when Emi closed her eyes for the last time, it was I who was left in the dark. I understood instantly what winter was like in Fairbanks, as I suffered an endless night and a cruel coldness for many months. Day after day, I felt like my world was dark, and I was blind. Inside, I stumbled around in that darkness of spirit. Outside, especially on a sunny day, my mind and my heart felt shrouded in inky blackness. If there was light at the end of this long, psychological tunnel, I couldn't see it. My Light had been taken away, so I stumbled in shock and grief again and again.

In contrast to my usually warm nature, I now found myself cold all the time, an emotional freeze emanating from the inside out. Nothing, not even blankets or hot drinks, warmed me. I shivered in bed all night long under a pile of blankets, wide awake. For months I worked on my recovery during my grief journey, and gradually light and warmth returned with each revelation I uncovered inside myself, but one thing was sorely lacking: a support group of lesbians and gays who had also suffered the loss of their loved one.

Ellen and I had spoken sadly about this lack in the Indianapolis LGBT community and elsewhere. So almost a year later, I was delightfully surprised when she invited me to a totally funded grief support group. Ellen and her partner, who worked in grief support within the Indiana University Health Network, had convinced the network supporters of this vital lack in the Circle City. Miraculously, they gained the funding necessary to organize an LGBT grief support group for six weeks! I could not have felt more grateful.

The invitation-only group met once a week in the early evening for two hours at an IU Health facility. The group consisted mainly of lesbians who had lost a parent, a sibling, or a child to various sicknesses or accidents. I was the only lesbian who had lost a partner. There were also a couple of gay men, including one who had lost his partner to cancer. Each person was grieving a unique loss and was seeking to cope with it in his or her own way. Lovingly and knowingly, Ellen and her partner developed, organized, and facilitated each session, which centered on a different facet of the grieving process each week. Naturally, each participant was on a different step of the grief journey, which made the sharing interesting and timely. I listened mindfully with deep understanding as each person responded to the topic of the evening's session. I spoke only when it was my turn, always concerned that I might cry. But crying was expected here as evidenced by the large boxes of tissues placed conveniently along the conference-sized discussion table, and most of the men and women did tear up as they spoke of their losses.

During the break in the middle of each session, there was an opportunity to speak individually with either therapist or any client in a more casual way. Again, I mostly listened to their conversations. I was that shy in large groups. During the sharing sessions, the topics for discussion highlighted loss, pain, insight, and healing. The group worked together during the therapeutic activities to open themselves to meditations on self-healing. Sometimes we worked in pairs or in small groups to implement fresh ideas and to express new understanding of the pain of loss from which we collectively suffered.

The six weeks passed much too fast for me, and I have to admit that the support group really helped to light the darkness in my mind and to warm my coldness of spirit. As I had believed, the opportunity to learn from other members of the LBGT community, people on their own grief journeys, brought me peace, solace, and insight, and I was blessed once again with mental light and emotional warmth.

Elizabeth Kidwell

If ever sun could split the night
And turn stark blackness into light

A blazing star of midnight mourn
Cascading down a face forlorn,

The miracle would not be known
Except by one who grieves alone.

For grief is singular to one
Who lives in darkness, outer sun,

Where beams can only pierce the soul
Like twilight on a grassy knoll,

Where shady gloom wields pride of place
Eclipsed by knowledge, inner space,

And stars of insight blaze above
The loss and lingering of a love.

When one day soon auroras rise
To shimmer brightness in the eyes,

Illuminate as clear as day
The midnight dungeon of my stay,

Then, light-released I hope to find
A joyous person heart and mind,

Allowing life to love once more
By simply opening the sun-lit door.

Chapter 24
Restored

They are called "triggers." No matter where I stood in my grief journey, one small object, one meaningful song, one soft, familiar fragrance, one sweet remembrance, one loving photo, one precious location, one favorite food, and BAM! I was right back in the thick of my sorrow again, not even meaning to be, overwhelmed by pain totally unexpected. I was hijacked by memory, helpless to respond in any way except sadness and tears. This is the mean thing that triggers do. I realized then, after a year of stumbling blindly around the house, that it would never be home to me again because its heart was missing. If I ever was to recover fully, I concluded, I needed to pack up, to sell this house of memories, and to rediscover my own heart, my own life. But Emi, I soon realized, had some unfinished business with me.

So it was that by the time I finally sat down to have that long-deferred talk with Emi about her loss of Beth and about her eventual death and my loss of her, she had already been gone for almost two years. I was approaching the last stages of emptying out the house and had at last arrived at the final two rooms on the second floor: my office and my bedroom. It had been over a year since I had spent much time in my office, so not much had changed since Emi died, other than the intermittent presence of daily rainbows.

I had already cleared the closet, so I decided to continue with my teacher's desk. On it sat a two-shelf oak book hutch where I had hastily stored Emi's five journals, the volumes Louise had placed lovingly in my hands just days after Emi died. Overwhelmed with sadness and deadlines, I had forgotten them until now. Their red covers embossed with gold designs immediately beckoned to me, so I sat down, took the first one from the shelf, and reverently opened it. Emi's familiar scritch-scratch cursive leaped out at me, and in my mind, I clearly heard her sad voice as I began to read. "I feel like I have been at sea for five years, and now I am finally sailing into port," she wrote in January 1988. "It has been a long journey, but it feels good to walk again on firm ground."

At last, I thought, here is the person I really needed to talk to, my Emi. No one understood better than she did about the loss and the pain that I had been going through. As I read her grief journal, I was surprised to find that she had emerged from her mental anguish just in time because she met me at a meeting for older lesbians less than one month later. Her timing could not have been more perfect. As far as I knew during the twenty-five years of our relationship, her journals sat unread on her bookshelf and then an additional two years on mine, just waiting for the time that I needed her words most, and thus it was that our journal conversations finally brought me into shore as well. Her familiar voice emerged from the pages as I began to read.

"My grief over Beth's loss came and went," she began, "over and over again. Eventually, few people wanted to talk to me about my pain and loss. Friends seemed uncomfortable and disappeared suddenly, assuming after a year or two that I was fully recovered from Beth's death, but I was far from recovered, and on some days, my loneliness seemed even worse. Her loss threw my life totally out of balance." Her words leapt from the page and thus began our long deferred conversation.

Yes, my Love, I understand, I mentally responded, speaking to her in my mind. Nothing has been in balance in my life since you left me. I miss you more than I ever thought possible. All during our life together, I dreaded that moment when you would take your last breath and leave me. Your loss hurt worse than any wound I had ever received. I never knew that anyone could survive pain this intense, but you knew it, didn't you? So many times you wanted to talk to me about it, but I was too frightened and too stubborn to listen. I know that you wanted to spare me this pain, but you knew from experience that there was no way you could do that for me, just as there was no way that Beth could have spared you.

I read on as Emi continued to speak to me. "Tears were nature's way of helping me to express and to release my pain. The resilience of the human spirit is truly amazing, I discovered. I learned that I had the ability to survive the three phases of the grieving process: numbness, suffering, and disorganization. Inevitably, as I began to recover, there was a long period of reorganization for me. My life as I had lived it was never the same again," she explained.

Emi, I told her in my heart, I find it very hard to sleep since you've been gone. Our doctor gave me a sleep aid to take when it is impossible to rest and I feel overwhelmed.

Emi's journal provided an answer for that, too, at the time for herself and now for me. "Sleep problems arise from the incredible strain of the psychological work that grief demands. Mourning, for me, created an overload, more stress than my mind could handle comfortably, either during sleep or in waking time. Insomnia is common for me, oh yes! It is important to rest in order to renew my energy, to keep up my strength, and to maintain my health, even though I am unable to sleep much. It's hard!"

Emi, I responded in my mind, I know now how hard it is. If I could just hold you once more, feel your warmth against me, your arms around me, make love and feel that magical passion we shared, I think that I could rest and perhaps sleep again. Even now I feel my desire for you build in me, but I don't know what to do with it.

Again, Emi had an answer born of personal experience. "Sensuality is deeply affected by grief. My sexual needs intensified along with other needs. I discovered that masturbation helped diminish my sexual tension and my feelings of frustration. Oh, yes! I have met new people who sometimes reach out to me, and then I feel important and cared about once again. Any special treatment feels enormously supportive to me and helps me to face the pain of my grief."

Emi, I confessed to her in my mind once more, I made some big mistakes by trying to take shortcuts in my grief. I doubled my pain by not being well enough or strong enough to take on new relationships. I wasn't thoroughly healed from the grief of your loss when I tried to fulfill my promise to you. I made a mess of things and extended my grief journey. My feelings were too raw to take on the additional burden of rejection.

Emi had an answer for that, too. "Loneliness and yearning are common problems in bereavement. Beth's death left a hole in my heart that I felt very deeply. I naturally believed that no one could ever fill that void. Because Beth was so special, I experienced her loss more keenly. As painful as it was, loneliness forced me to acknowledge the truth and the depth of my loss, which has left me with a painful gap in my life. Since my grief was so painful and devastating, I pushed myself to finish grieving long before I was ready. The real truth is that I will heal in my own unique time frame."

After reading her words, I suddenly recalled a devastating event that Emi had shared with me shortly after we found each other. Four years into her grief journey, Emi had reconnected with a male colleague in the military intelligence service. While the man was in Indianapolis, he and Emi went out to dinner and then returned to Emi's house for a nightcap. One drink led to another until they were both quite intoxicated, she had shared with me. Then the man, whom she had respected and trusted, made sexual advances toward her. When she refused his unwanted advances, he became angry, and in his drunken state, he overpowered Emi, held her down, and forcibly raped her on the couch in her own living room. Rape, for Emi, was an act of war. She became so enraged at what he had done that she vowed never to see him again and to give up alcohol. Consequently, during our years together, we never kept hard liquor in the house. Recalling this, I realized in sad amazement that Emi, too, had tried to take a short-cut in her grief journey with catastrophic results. Desperate loneliness that followed the loss of a great love, I understood, had caused us both to take a personally hurtful path.

In 1984, one year after Beth's death, Emi took a day trip to Brookville, Indiana, where she had begun her teaching career forty years before. "I realized," she wrote, "that I do not like the person I have become in the classroom, so it is really time, or past time, to leave. Retirement is right. I really loved being in Brookville, my first teaching experience. I perfected my skills here and in Delphi. My best teaching was in Hammond and at Marshall in Indianapolis. This day and its glorious fall weather and landscapes and thoughts gave me some new peace that was so needed." So it was that Emi retired at age sixty after forty years of teaching. How she survived that one year at Arlington High School, I will never understand because I know that the emptiness she felt left her so little to give her students. I was very grateful that when Emi left this world, I was already fully retired after forty years of teaching and three years of teacher supervision. No way could I have continued giving to anyone while suffering such total emptiness, but then Emi was always stronger than I was. "For every wound," she wrote, "there is the ointment of time."

So it happened that the journals of Emi's grief journey and the conversations I finally had with her in my mind allowed me to imagine the possibilities that life still had in store for me, as it had opened the future for her. Thirty years ago, when we first declared our love for each other, Emi believed that she would live for six to eight years at best.

I responded immediately. "That is not enough for me. Beth had thirty years with you," I insisted, "and I want the same."

"All right," she agreed with amused determination, "thirty years it is. I will do my best to make it!"

"And I'll be helping you," I promised, taking her into my arms and sealing our vows with a kiss.

"And after thirty years," she continued with a wink and sly smile, "if everything goes well, we can renew our promise for a longer time!" The squeeze we gave each other melded us together for life.

As it turned out, Emi gave me twenty-five of the most love-packed, fun-filled years of my existence. During our life together, we honestly felt like two children, delighting in exploring our inner and outer worlds. While health challenges sometimes slowed our pace, these setbacks never stopped us, and as soon as we recovered, we would pick up the pace and blaze on! We packed a lifetime of love into those twenty-five years. For that, I am grateful.

When television personality, George Burns lost his beloved wife Gracie Allen, he wrote, "Get up each morning to something. If you are afraid of your future, you have no present." Emi had written this quotation in her journal. Taking his advice and hers, I make plans for each day. I try to stay active and to have at least one activity to look forward to.

One of the greatest strengths of my relationship with Emi lay in our perception of it. We never considered ourselves two halves of a whole. If we had, I would now be broken forever. Instead, we always maintained our independence together. We constantly thought of ourselves as two separate, whole, and complete people who shared our lives, loves, and interests. Giving each other space allowed us to enrich each other with our individual interests and discoveries. Emi enjoyed her Elderhostels, war games, enrichment classes at Butler University, IU Mini-med School, Oasis, and Heritage Place. I shared my family trips to my parents' ranch in California, my family reunions, multiple family trips, and adventures with old friends. Often Emi accompanied me and enjoyed time with my family and friends as I did with hers. In addition, I shared new information gained during mandatory educational workshops and conventions, and Emi, always a magnificent teacher, even graced my classroom with enrichment presentations that my students loved!

The majority of the time, however, the two of us traveled widely or attended classes together. Like a team of explorers, we reveled in every wonder we experienced, never losing our thirst for adventures! Emi and I were rich beyond all measure, understanding how blessed we were to have found each other. I like to believe that to even out the perils, the evils, and the pain she suffered during her national service, and as thanksgiving for her forty years of teaching, Emi was granted two relationships of a lifetime: fifty-five years of unconditional love from two lively and devoted women.

As for me, I am truly grateful for my twenty-five years with Emi. I was always so proud of her. She never knew a stranger, but she would strike up a conversation with anyone she met, teaching me by example not to be so shy. Like two wide-eyed children, we sought after knowledge, beauty, everyday miracles, and the wonders of Mother Earth. With Emi's inspiration and love inside me, I will continue to be dazzled by the wondrous outside world and also by the incredibly mystifying world that I carry within. The change is, that now, I see through our eyes!

Elizabeth Kidwell

As if love were not enough for me,
The most precious gift you bore
Was the ability to laugh and sing
And dance, and want for more.

You taught me well that life has joy
In the moments that we share,
So even when we were apart,
Your love was always there.

You showed me treasures of the world
And enjoyed them through my eyes,
You named each bird, the flying gems
That soared through azure skies.

I read to you and sang to you;
You listened, silent love,
Your glance was healing to my heart.
You fit me like a glove.

Hand in hand we sought for life
With boundless energy;
We swam and played and traveled far
To give youth back to me.

And when with childlike face I smiled
And thanked you for this prize,
You hugged me close, then let me go
And made me realize

Wounded Wings

That childhood is no finite gift.
It grows long in each mind
And beams at me from people's lives
Whenever I am kind.

I recognized the child in you,
And you set mine so free,
That now as I go on alone,
Your child lives on in me.

Chapter 25
Postcards

Gradually over time, I could see that Emi was losing ground each day, and it tore me up. "I am sorry I got old," she would apologize to me, aware that as she relinquished more and more responsibilities, I took them on. It broke my heart when she said those words because the relentless onslaught of time was nothing she could help. I was careful never to complain and always to smile when faced with new challenges.

One freedom that Emi valued above all others was her independence to travel. She had worn out several cars and bicycles from her sojourns across North America and Europe. She had always driven a stick shift automobile, but when she turned eighty, her vintage VW Golf became a problem for her to drive. I had not ridden with her for quite some time, so one summer morning I had her drive us to Eagle Creek Park for a birdwatching picnic. On the way, Emi struggled while working the foot pedals because of her neuropathy. I held my breath most of the way, especially concerned when she had to shift into a new gear. Over our picnic lunch, we discussed the difficulty she had shifting because of the numbness and the tingling in her feet. Emi hung her head sadly and said, "I guess it is time for me to stop driving."

"Nonsense," I replied happily, gifting her with my best smile, "it is just time for you to get a new car that is easier to drive!" Emi raised her head and grinned at me, relief and joy lighting up her face. "If you can give up manual transmission," I teased her, "we can trade in your Golf for a good used car with automatic transmission, power steering, and power brakes. Let's go home and call Sparky at the VW dealership to see if he has such a car taken in trade. If you don't mind, though, I would like to drive home. It pained me to watch you struggle with those pedals."

"I would love for you to drive home," Emi replied excitedly, "and then we can call Sparky!"

Sparky was a sweet World War II veteran, who worked part time at the VW dealership. He had handled my last automobile purchase, and Emi had struck up a conversation with him then. As soon as we returned home, I telephone him and explained our dilemma. "Emi needs a good, reliable used car, easy to drive with automatic transmission, power steering and brakes," I told him. Sparky promised to check right away and to call us back.

Within the hour we heard from him. "I think we have the perfect car for Emi," he began. "It is a 2003 Chevy Prism with all the features you have mentioned. Fortunately, 2003 was the last year that Chevrolet produced the Prism. It is a clean, one-owner, trade-in vehicle, and it is in great condition. It has less than 47,000 miles on it, and the car's previous owner was a minister."

I turned to tell Emi, and her face lit up. "Can we go see it today?" she asked.

"Sparky, we'll be there in an hour," I told him before hanging up. On the Internet I investigated the Chevy Prism on the Kelly Blue Book website and was pleased to discover that it was a great, reliable, used automobile, and the price they were asking was right in line with its suggested value. I drove Emi to the VW dealership in her old Golf, which we would trade in. Emi fell in love with the teal green four-door Prism as soon as she test drove it! After completing the paper work, we agreed to return the next day to pick up her new used car and to trade in her Golf. For the next four years, Emi happily reveled in the freedom and the independence that her new car afforded her.

One fall evening two years later, I was quietly focused on school work at home, when the telephone rang. Emi had driven herself to Riley Hospital for Children, where IU Medical Center held the monthly Mini-Med School lectures. Always the scientist, Emi had attended these sessions for years. Absorbed in schoolwork, I hadn't noticed that Emi was a half hour late getting home, so it was a surprise when the telephone rang and I heard her voice coming to me from her cell phone. Hearing her strange tone, I realized immediately that something was amiss. "I am lost," she confessed, sounding bewildered.

"Do you have any clue where you might be?" I asked softly, trying to control my alarm.

"I think that I am on the west side near the airport," she answered, unsure of herself. "I am going to pull into the well-lit gas station up ahead and ask for directions. I wanted to let you know because it will probably take me another half hour to get home, and I didn't want you to worry."

But worry I did until she arrived home at 10:00 p.m. A discussion about Emi's problem with night driving ensued, even despite her two cataract surgeries, and from then on, I became her evening chauffeur. For the next two years, Emi continued to enjoy the freedom that driving provided her in the daylight, but during her eighty-fourth year, everything changed.

One spring day I had arrived home from school earlier than usual, and Emi was still napping. Suddenly, the telephone rang, and I answered it quickly so the ringing wouldn't wake Emi. I was surprised to hear the familiar voice of Denise, our doctor's nurse, asking for me. I was immediately curious since neither of us had appointments scheduled. "Ellie, the doctor asked me to call you," she said sounding serious. "She just received a phone call from Maryanne, Emi's therapist. She told her that Emi had a session with her this morning. She said that when they sat down to begin their discussion, Emi told her that she had locked her keys in her car with the motor running. They called Triple A right away so that the serviceman would arrive in the parking garage by the time their session ended. After an hour, she walked Emi to her car in the garage. There was the Triple A guy standing at Emi's car scratching his head. The car was running as Emi had said, but all of the windows were rolled down! Emi was confused and embarrassed, but she asked Maryanne not to tell you. However, Maryanne thought that someone should know, so she called our office to tell the doctor. Doctor Kathy told me to call you right away."

I was stunned at this news because Emi and I never kept secrets from each other, but it was obvious that Emi had suffered some kind of little stroke and had become confused. "Thank you, Denise," I said sadly, "and thank Dr. Kathy for letting me know right away. I will talk to Emi." I hung up and took a deep breath as I realized how serious and difficult my next conversation with my beloved woman would be. A few moments later, I heard Emi stirring in her bedroom, but I decided to postpone this unwanted discussion until after dinner, when she would be fully awake and relaxed. Following our meal in the kitchen, I cleared the table and then sat back down taking Emi's hands in my own. I gazed into her soft, brown eyes with love and described for her the telephone call which I had received. Emi's eyes grew wide as she realized her secret was out. "Technically," I explained, "Maryanne did not tell me, but Dr. Kathy felt it was serious enough to let me know right away. You know that I love you more than anything and want to keep you safe. What happened today is troubling to me," I continued, "and it must be to you, too. We need to face the fact that your head injuries over the years may now be causing some difficulties in your mental perception. We need to consider that for your safety and the safety of others, this might be the best time for you to give up driving."

Emi looked down at our hands sadly, but responded in earnest, "I don't agree. I was able to drive home safely."

"But Emi," I countered, "this incident occurred after you arrived at your destination. What if the next episode of confusion happens while you are driving? You would be devastated if you caused an accident that injured or even killed someone, and I would be destroyed if you died in an accident." Emi hung her head sadly, defeated. "Look," I promised, "I will drive you to any place you want to go. I will even try to get home early from school to be your personal chauffeur." It look another half hour of logical persuasion, but eventually, my concerns wore Emi down, and I got her to admit that maybe not driving was for the best. I decided not to hide her car keys, but out of respect for her, to leave them in the silver dish near the front door where they had always been kept.

The next day, I called Emi from school during my lunch break to see how she was doing. There was no answer. Puzzled and concerned, I dialed again to make sure, and then I telephoned my neighbor across the street who worked out of her home. "Emi is not answering the phone," I explained. "Could you do me a big favor and peek in the garage door window to see if her car is in there?"

"No problem," my neighbor replied. "I'll just run across the street and see. Stay on the line." It didn't take her long to inform me that Emi's car was gone!

"Thank you," I told her, hanging up exasperated and disappointed. That afternoon when I returned home, I confronted Emi. "I called you today at noon, and you were not home. Did you go somewhere in your car?"

"Yes," she told me truthfully. "I had an errand to run."

Well after that, I never confronted her again about the car. I remembered how my oldest sister had taken my father's car keys away from him when his heart began to fail and he became confused. After his death months later, I discovered a set of keys in his bedroom closet, carefully tucked into his jacket pocket, where he always kept them. Octogenarians are stubborn, I had concluded then, realizing ultimately that they will always find a way! So I just assumed that during the day, Emi drove herself various places, but I never took her keys away, and I never questioned her. I did occasionally check her mileage gauge to make sure that the trips were short. Eventually, however, I drove her to more and more places, and I also alternated driving our two cars to work to keep the batteries charged. A year or so later, I suggested that Emi sell her Prism while she could still make money on it. A friend needed a reliable used car for her daughter, and Emi made $2,500 on it. I knew that it was difficult for Emi to relinquish her freedom, but by this time she had acquiesced to the wisdom of it.

Eventually, it became exhausting for Emi to travel long distances. The last trip we took together was a thousand mile round trip to the Stratford Festival in Ontario, Canada. It was our second trip to Stratford, a shorter one this time. Years ago we enjoyed our Elderhostel there on English theatre, and we had always planned to return. This time we decided to see six stage plays, two plays a day for three days. We would drive there in one day and then return home in one day. To make the trip more comfortable for Emi, I outfitted my VW Jetta Wagon with a power inverter that could run off the AC power of my car so that I could hook up her CPAP for naps on the road. It worked beautifully as I tucked her into the passenger side with pillows and a comforter, seat reclined, and her breathing machine with the power inverter resting on the back seat. She was able to sleep peacefully while I drove.

Our schedule while in Stratford was simple: wake up, have breakfast in the hotel restaurant, attend a matinee performance, return to the hotel for Emi's nap, have dinner, take in an evening performance, return to the hotel, and retire for the night. That was all the energy that Emi could muster, but she loved every minute of our mini-vacation and never complained! I pushed her everywhere in her collapsible wheelchair, which we had brought with us so that she could conserve her energy and enjoy each play. The day after we arrived home, the customary commemorative postcard was delivered by mail. It was a beautiful scene of the Festival Theatre in Stratford, Ontario, taken at dusk. The circular theatre was lit up against the turquoise sky, mirrored like a dream in Lake Victoria! Emi had bought it at the hotel and mailed it from the hotel desk in the lobby. On it she had written, "Darling, you and this trip mean the world to me. Thank you for making it happen! I love you!"

Postcards are a photographer's stop-time vision of beauty to commemorate a place swarming with it. Emi loved to celebrate our travels with postcards and life maps. After she died, I discovered over a hundred unsent postcards in her desk purchased during her travels with Beth and with me, spanning fifty-five years. My sister Louise had also boxed up an equal number of Emi's unsent greeting cards. I kept both collections when I moved and eventually put them to good use. My younger sister Elaine lives in a nursing home in California, suffering from Parkinson's disease. At least once a week or more I send her a card and a short letter, and inside the card I include one of Emi's postcards. On the back of each card, I write an explanation or a memory about the location. Many of the postcards feature wild animals or birds as well as lovely scenery or impressive architecture. Because Emi had once taken an architectural drawing class in school, she recognized the art and the beauty in man-made structures as well as in nature.

For the first two years following Emi's death, I stuck close to home because grief had rolled me into a ball of pain. It was difficult to see the wonders of life during that time because my vision was turned inward as I tried to make sense of the emptiness I felt. Gradually as the months crawled by, Emi's promise, her indomitable spirit, and the love of my family and friends pulled me from the brink of sadness back into the light and warmth of reality and life. My vision began to clear, and I could tolerate the life going on all around me once again, and even become a part of it. I was determined to make up for the living I had lost by creating a new life road map. While I understood that as spirit, Emi could travel anywhere in the universe she chose, her postcards never ended. Now the postcards were living ones: beautiful sunrises and sunsets, brilliantly white moon, planets, and stars in the inky blackness of space, the changing trees by season, and wildlife and birds in my own backyard. On my part, I was determined to continue to share with her the world as seen through my eyes and to take her along in my heart. What followed were not just journeys to places, but also into the lives of people, and into my own mind as well.

It took me two difficult years to recover my desire to travel alone again, but recover I did, due in part to Emi's pioneer wanderlust combined in spirit with my own personal resilience, finally recovered during my practice of mindfulness meditation and peaceful breathing. I discovered in my core, that living so long with Emi had made me brave, too! She had always encouraged me "to take the roads less traveled," to seek fresh wonders, to collect states along the way, and to create a new bucket list. My iPad makes postcards unnecessary as I now create photos using my own vision inspired by Emi's. In my present wanderings, I seek out places that Emi and I never visited together.

My first long road trip without Emi was back to Florida, where we had enjoyed many warm spring breaks. It was winter now though, and as it turned out, the worst winter, the snowiest and coldest that Indianapolis had experienced since the 1930s! Talk about great timing! The first city in Florida I wanted to explore was the oldest city in the nation, St. Augustine. Highlights of my time in St. Augustine included visits to the St. Augustine Alligator Farm and Zoological Park and to the fortress Castillo de San Marcos.

The albino alligators at the Alligator Farm were high on my list since I had never seen one before. The attendant assured me that the white alligators were quite numerous at birth, but that their white skin made camouflage impossible in the wild, so most of the babies became food for predators shortly after hatching. The two five-foot, albino alligators in captivity at the Alligator Farm were lodged there for their own protection, affording sightseers a rare opportunity to view them up close.

As a military historian, Emi had been a collector of forts, so of course, I took her in my heart when I visited Castillo de San Marcos, the oldest masonry fort in the United States and the only standing military structure from the seventeenth century. A star fort with four bastions, it is 345 years old, begun in 1672 and built of coquina, a soft native limestone formed by the Atlantic Ocean from crushed shells. The construction rocks had been harvested in the nearby area. The coquina absorbed or deflected enemy projectiles and was also fireproof. I knew that Emi would approve of this old fortress. It was my postcard to her!

On the Caribbean side of Florida, I visited Homosassa Springs Wildlife State Park, a 210 acre wildlife preserve operated by the state of Florida with the help of at least 350 volunteers. It is one of the best wildlife rehabilitation centers in our nation. Its Felburn wildlife case center is a cutting edge, state of the art facility which supports the manatee rehabilitation center for the care of sick and injured manatees. There I saw six manatees, up close and personal, drifting peacefully on the Homosassa River like giant baked potatoes! The park was inspiring, a good location to view wintering wild birds, who flew freely by the dozens into the enclosures of birds who were wounded and couldn't fly.

On the way to the Florida Keys, I had a rare look at the wild and illusive Florida Panther, peacefully lapping water with its soft pink tongue from a wide creek. The state animal of Florida, the Florida Panther is an endangered population of cougar living in the swamps and forests of south Florida. My sighting reminded me that Emi had seen a Florida Panther just months before she met me, and she had told me about it while the event was still fresh in her mind. She said that she was birdwatching alone in the Everglades when she discovered the Panther observing her from a large branch of a nearby tree! She told me that the cougar was lying down and had probably already eaten that day because it didn't seem particularly interested in her. Twenty-seven years later, I saw my cougar. Since there are only about 230 panthers remaining in Florida, I felt particularly lucky, and who is to say that my Emi did not inspire that panther to make that special appearance?

During a short stay on Long Key, I visited Long Key State Park and hiked the Layton Trail on the bay side of the park. There along the beach, I was favored with another sighting of both the tricolored heron and the little blue heron, two species of large water birds I had seen with Emi during our vacation years before on Sanibel Island. As I stood on the shore of Long Key, I suddenly realized that I was looking at a large bird I had never seen before. I put Emi's binoculars up to my eyes to see the bird more clearly. Then I consulted my field guide. It was a reddish egret, who was too busy canopy feeding to be bothered with me. So I got a great look at my next lifer bird demonstrating for me its clever feeding habit of raising its wings to create shade for the fish, who cluelessly gather at its feet and become an easy meal!

In the following two years, I drove twice to California and back, adding Idaho and Montana to my growing bucket list of states. While many of my adventures included short visits to relatives and friends along the way, I pleasantly discovered that I enjoyed my own company as well! On my second road trip to California, I drove through Nebraska to the Platte River Valley. I stopped in Kearney and visited the Rowe Bird Sanctuary, where each spring over 500,000 sandhill cranes, 80% of the world's population, gather each March during one of the earth's greatest migrations. Emi and I had watched a documentary on TV about this place many years before. So my bucket list plan is to return some year in March for this lifetime spectacle. Emi would have loved it, and I know that she will be right there with me in spirit, another postcard for her.

On the way home from California that same fall, I stopped to visit two dear friends in Fernley, Nevada. They surprised me with a short road trip to Pyramid Lake located on the Pyramid Lake Indian Reservation about fifty miles northeast of Reno. Tribal members are direct descendants of the Northern Paiute people. The lake is named for the large pyramid tufa rock rising from its waters and other formations along it shores formed from calcium carbonate. I was astounded by the desert lake's beauty and by its striking deep blue color as it winked and danced and sparkled in the sunlight before me. While 890 feet deep and 27 miles long, Pyramid Lake is a small remnant of Pleistocene Lake Lahontan, fed solely by water carried along the Truckee River from Lake Tahoe. While standing on its ancient shores, I felt Emi beside me, gazing at this amazing place through my eyes.

My mission for the remaining years of my life is to continue exploring unfamiliar places, to meet new people, and to enjoy the wonders of life. I will revive our quest "to walk in beauty," to experience and to appreciate the loveliness in every person, in every destination, and in all wonders of the natural world for the remainder of my life. If I cannot see the beauty, then I need to look closer, using my inner vision. Together, Emi and I understood this truth profoundly. Once my fog of sorrow finally cleared, I discovered how to rise above my loss and my grief, to look beyond my loneliness, and to fly again on wounded wings. Love made me just that strong.

Elizabeth Kidwell

Whenever we were wondering
Across this sacred land,
You always took the time to write
And sign with your own hand

A postcard of our memories
To send back home from you,
A priceless record of our trip
When all the traveling's through.

I saved them in a little box,
Which filled up through the years
And as I read them once again,
My eyes overflowed with tears.

The beauty and the daring
And the fun we always had
Only makes me miss you more.
The memories make me sad.

I still have love for viewing life
Though I stay close to home,
But you are free to travel now
Wherever you wish to roam.

But as for me, I stay right here
And watch, though it is hard,
For that one day when the mailman
Might deliver that next postcard.

Wounded Wings

Eventually, though, I realized
Through countless, bitter tears
That this is not the road of life
To follow through the years.

I need to discover beauty
As I travel through this land.
My eyes become your vision
As we wander hand in hand.

Living always inside of me,
Your spirit roaming wide,
I'll honor you by living well.
Your love will be my guide.

Chapter 26
Showered

Emi hated to shop, but she loved to give presents. I discovered early in our relationship that she used mail ordering to secure gifts for me and for others. Almost every weekend's visit with her included a gift, as if the generosity of her love, time, laughter, and knowledge were not priceless enough. Inevitably, an item would catch her fancy in one of her many catalogs, and before I knew it, I was the proud owner. After months of being showered with presents, and fearful of becoming a hoarder myself every time I brought a gift home, I decided it was time to explain my simple lifestyle and philosophy of life to Emi.

The best time to do this was after love making. We usually had some of our most heartfelt conversations when our minds and hearts were centered completely on each other. I realized that this precious time would be the perfect opportunity to discuss the topic of generosity and to explain to Emi what I valued above all. So one day as we lay side by side in bed very happy with each other, I spoke from my heart. "Emi, you know that I love you completely," I began tentatively, very concerned about hurting her feelings.

"Yes," she replied immediately, her brown eyes flashing, "and I love you." She gave me a little squeeze with her strong, nut-brown arms.

"Well," I explained, "I wanted to share with you my feelings about your generosity."

At these words, Emi's eyebrows shot up; her eyes widened, and she grinned at me mischievously! "I can hardly wait," she teased.

"You know that I love the gifts you give me," I began unflustered, my eyes caressing hers, "because they come from you, but I am not comfortable owning so much stuff. You already give me your precious love and your time, and your knowledge about nature and birds. Those gifts cannot be bought because they come from your heart and mind, and they only fill up space in mine. The fabulous stories you share with me about your life adventures and the people you love are priceless to me. These are the gifts you give me whenever we are together, and I value them the most."

"Yes, Darling," she replied, "I understand. I value the love you give me and the gift of yourself beyond everything."

"I don't really need things," I continued, "although every gift you have given me carries a memory as well. I would rather spend our money making memories through traveling, gathering with friends, and celebrating our lives together."

Emi pulled me close again. "Darling, we will do just that, though occasionally I would like to buy you a small souvenir of our journeys together. Would that be all right?"

"Absolutely!" I replied happily, snuggling even closer. From then on, Emi's "small souvenirs" took the form of little Zuni fetishes, which I began collecting during a road trip in Massachusetts. I was attracted to them because each fetish combined my love of beautiful rocks, animals, tiny sculptures, and Native American teaching. The Zuni people believed that these little polished figures, created by skilled artists, contained the spirit of the animals. I discovered later that Emi had cheated somewhat because on our trips, she would buy not one fetish, but four at a time, giving me one as a homecoming gift and concealing the other three. On our anniversary, winter solstice, and my birthday each year, a fetish would mysteriously appear in a colorful, wrapped gift box! Emi just couldn't help herself, and her thoughtfulness only made me love her more. Besides, she only had to shop once so it worked for her, too! By the time Emi could no longer travel, I owned over a hundred of those sacred figures and several leaded glass cases where they were displayed.

Up until the time of our discussion, Emi had paid for our short weekend excursions herself. Now, however, I insisted that that we share the expenses 50-50. Emi agreed after a short protest that she made more money retired than I did teaching full time. I knew that she liked taking care of me, but I wanted an equal partnership. I was firm on that.

Elizabeth Kidwell

When Emi invited me to move in with her following my cancer surgery in 1994, I insisted on a legal agreement regarding the operation of household expenses. I told Emi that I would not move in until we had a signed and witnessed document in hand. She readily agreed, and after I sold my house and most of my furniture, we signed a legal paper drawn up by her attorney, and we became a family! We opened a joint checking account at a separate bank. Each month we deposited an equal amount of money, and all bills, food, utilities, taxes, repairs, and insurance were paid from that account. We shared responsibilities and grew even closer because of it. When occasionally I came up short because of my private school teacher's salary, Emi would cover for me until I could pay it back, and pay her back, I did! I loved Emi enough never to take advantage of her great love for me and her matchless generosity. Every trip we took from then on was a joint expense. We took turns paying for gas, food, lodging, and sight-seeing excursions. Emi kept receipts and records of what we each spent in two separate envelopes. When we returned home, Emi tallied up our totals, and the low person paid the difference to the other.

I loved that our life together was equal and fair, and I always believed that secretly, Emi was proud of my decision to pay my fair share, although she continued to contend that she could afford to pay more. As the years flew by, I was able to save some money each month for my retirement years, understanding that when those years finally arrived, I would probably be on my own.

After Emi died, I lived in the large house alone for two years, but without Emi, it no longer seemed like a home to me. As I cleaned it out, the emptier it became, the emptier I felt. Retired now, alone, and living on Social Security, I could no longer afford the taxes and the upkeep on this beautiful house in Butler-Tarkington. I sold the house to a special couple whom Emi had known and loved for thirty years. I knew she would approve. Eventually, I bought a small, single level patio home in the more affordable southeast side of Indianapolis. I knew that this house was where I was supposed to be when I realized that it was the only home of the twenty-four on the circle that boasted a white eagle hanging above the garage door. Emi had always been my eagle, and it seemed like a sign from her, so I called my new house "White Eagle," a bird sacred to native people. Like a proper Native American dwelling, the sun rises at my east-facing front door each morning and sets at my back west-facing door every evening. Sitting on my back screened-in porch affords me open views of two large, gently-rolling fields and two wooded areas beyond, where I often catch sight of numerous squirrels, deer, coyotes, raccoons, rabbits, and coy-wolves. The fields and woods are rich with bird life: eastern bluebirds, red-tailed hawks, red-headed woodpeckers, pileated woodpeckers, great-horned owls, tree swallows, Canada geese, cardinals, field sparrows, yellow-shafted flickers, robins, eastern kingbirds, red-winged blackbirds, killdeer, mockingbirds, great blue herons, sandhill cranes, and bald eagles. And I don't have to go looking for them. They come to me! Most of all, I have an unobstructed view of the sunset each evening in all its colorful splendor. No two sunsets have ever been the same, thanks to Sky Painter, and I believe that Emi would have loved this home for me. Sometimes, I feel her approving presence, especially when an unexpected bird appears, like the white shouldered tanager from Central America!

Four years after Emi's death, when my grief had become manageable and my life peaceful, I fulfilled my last promise to my sweet woman. I took Emi's ashes and drove with my guardian friends, Ann and Richard, to Turkey Run State Park for the 100th Anniversary celebration of the founding of Indiana's State Park system, an occasion Emi would not have missed, and as it turned out, she didn't have to. After all the ceremonies were completed and the crowd dispersed, Ann, Richard, and I returned to the car for Emi's backpack. Quietly, we descended Trail 6 behind the cabins to Sugar Creek. It was blissfully silent except for appropriate soft birdsong overhead. Richard removed Emi's ashes from the backpack, still nestled in the clear plastic bag, and handed them to me. Lovingly and respectfully, as my friends watched, I walked along the bank of Sugar Creek until I came to the deepest, quiet pool of water nestled against a large limestone outcrop. I pictured in my mind a small, wiry child, splashing with happy abandon in her favorite place, surrounded by the total freedom of nature's beauty. Only then did I let go of the physical remains of the love of my life, watching sadly as she blended with the sand, and crying softly once again, as I am crying now.

Though Emi is no longer with me physically, the priceless memories we shared are fresh in my mind, and sometimes even feel palpable. However, she would never wish me to live completely in the past, I know. Occasionally, when a bird or an animal appears unexpectedly to jolt me into the present, I understand that Emi's sweet spirit is with me, encouraging me to continue living life to the fullest. Using the dynamic example she set for me while she was alive, I live on in her honor, volunteering my services, traveling to new places, visiting old friends and making new ones, learning new skills, keeping my body strong, and always reading, writing, and learning. Our life together was so incredibly rich, fine, and full, that now, having survived the shock of loss, I am blessed with the richness of our shared, breathtaking memories!

Wounded Wings

All I did was love you,
And the gifts rained down:
Silk and gold, silver and diamonds.
"This is too expensive," I objected.
"Love is priceless," you answered.

All I did was love you,
And the adventures began:
Mountains, oceans, forests, islands.
"But you have been here before," I protested.
"I see it anew through your eyes," you explained.

All I did was love you,
And there was a flood of your friends:
War gamers, birders, neighbors, students.
"There are so many people," I announced shyly.
"They will be your friends also," you insisted.

All I did was love you,
And the world opened up:
Birds, animals, trees, flowers, life.
"There is so much to learn," I announced.
"I will be your teacher," you offered.

Elizabeth Kidwell

All I did was love you,
But a hail of ailments blasted down on your
Legs, feet, eyes, ears, breast, heart, and mind.
"I am sorry I got old," you apologized.
"You are like fine wine and cheese," I maintained.

All I did was love you,
But silent lightning crashed down, taking you
And leaving me showered, rich in people, life, knowledge.
"I have had the world, best of everything," you wrote.
"And I have had more," I whispered, "because I love you."

Chapter 27
No Words

There are no words to capture
Everything you are to me:
A whisper in the darkness
On its voyage to be free,

A sunbeam on the forest floor,
Single, shining ray,
A cloud that drifts toward sunset
Arms outstretched to catch the day.

You are the single leaf that clings
To a tree's bare bones in fall,
But softly flutters to the ground
When snowflakes come to call.

You are the songbird's symphony
When morning mists arise,
The deep-blue endlessness of space,
The glory in my eyes.

You are the sparkling sunrise
Shattering my last reserve.
You are the mountain summit,
Every gift that I deserve.

I have no words to tell you,
Silent eagle, lost in flight,
That you have brought me endless day
And conquered endless night.

www.ingramcontent.com/pod-product-compliance
Lightning Source LLC
Chambersburg PA
CBHW050316120526
44592CB00014B/1929